Identity Governance and Administration (IGA):
From zero to hero

James Relington

DEDICATION

To all cybersecurity professionals. Your commitment to protecting access, enforcing governance, and navigating the complexities of identity management is invaluable. May this work serve as a guide and inspiration in your ongoing efforts to create a more secure and compliant future.

AKNOWLEDGEMENTS

I extend my deepest gratitude to everyone who contributed to the creation of this book. To my colleagues and mentors in the field of identity governance, your insights and expertise have been invaluable. To my friends and family, your unwavering support and encouragement have made this journey possible. To the professionals and innovators dedicated to securing digital identities, your work continues to inspire and shape the future of cybersecurity. This book is a reflection of collective knowledge, and I am grateful to all who have played a role in its development.

Introduction to Identity Governance and Administration (IGA)

Identity Governance and Administration (IGA) is a critical component of modern cybersecurity and IT management. It encompasses policies, processes, and technologies designed to ensure that the right individuals have appropriate access to an organization's systems, applications, and data. As enterprises grow and their IT environments become more complex, managing identities and access rights becomes increasingly challenging. IGA provides a structured approach to managing digital identities, improving security, maintaining compliance, and increasing operational efficiency.

The Importance of IGA in Today's Digital Landscape

Organizations operate in an era where digital transformation is accelerating. Cloud computing, remote work, and the proliferation of software-as-a-service (SaaS) applications have expanded the attack surface for cyber threats. Without a well-implemented IGA strategy, businesses face risks such as unauthorized access, data breaches, and non-compliance with regulatory requirements. IGA helps mitigate these risks by enforcing identity policies, automating access provisioning and de-provisioning, and ensuring continuous monitoring of user activities.

Regulatory compliance is another driving force behind IGA adoption. Various laws and industry regulations, such as the General Data Protection Regulation (GDPR), the Sarbanes-Oxley Act (SOX), and the Health Insurance Portability and Accountability Act (HIPAA), mandate strict controls over user access to sensitive data. IGA solutions help organizations comply with these requirements by providing audit trails, enforcing role-based access controls, and ensuring periodic access reviews.

Core Components of IGA

IGA consists of two primary components: identity governance and identity administration.

1. Identity Governance

Identity governance focuses on policies and oversight related to user access. It ensures that identity-related decisions align with business rules and regulatory requirements. Key elements of identity governance include:

- **Access Certification:** Regular reviews of user access to confirm that only authorized individuals have privileges.
- **Policy Management:** Defining and enforcing access policies across the organization.
- **Audit and Compliance Reporting:** Tracking identity and access-related activities to demonstrate compliance with security and regulatory standards.

2. Identity Administration

Identity administration deals with the operational aspects of managing user identities. It involves:

- **User Provisioning and De-Provisioning:** Automating the creation and removal of user accounts based on their role and employment status.
- **Role-Based Access Control (RBAC):** Assigning permissions based on job functions to streamline access management.
- **Self-Service Access Requests:** Allowing users to request access to resources while ensuring proper approvals and governance.

By integrating governance with administration, IGA provides a holistic approach to managing digital identities securely and efficiently.

Benefits of Implementing IGA

The adoption of an IGA framework brings multiple benefits to an organization, including enhanced security, regulatory compliance, and operational efficiency.

1. Improved Security Posture

With automated provisioning and de-provisioning, IGA ensures that users only have access to necessary resources for their job functions.

It also minimizes the risk of insider threats by enforcing strict access controls and monitoring identity-related activities.

2. Regulatory Compliance
Organizations must adhere to various data protection and security regulations. IGA solutions provide the necessary audit trails, reports, and enforcement mechanisms to ensure compliance. This helps organizations avoid costly fines and reputational damage.

3. Increased Efficiency and Productivity
Manual identity management processes can be time-consuming and prone to errors. IGA automates these processes, reducing administrative overhead and enabling IT teams to focus on strategic initiatives rather than routine access management tasks.

4. Enhanced User Experience
A well-implemented IGA solution streamlines access requests and approvals, reducing the time users wait to gain access to required applications. This leads to improved productivity and a better overall user experience.

Implementing an Effective IGA Strategy

For organizations looking to implement IGA, a well-planned strategy is essential. The following steps can help ensure successful deployment:

1. Define Business Requirements
Understanding business objectives, compliance requirements, and security needs is crucial for developing an effective IGA framework. Organizations should identify key stakeholders and align their IGA strategy with overall business goals.

2. Choose the Right IGA Solution
Selecting an IGA platform that integrates well with existing IT infrastructure is essential. Organizations should consider factors such as scalability, automation capabilities, and integration with cloud and on-premises applications.

3. Establish Governance Policies

Clearly defined policies for user access, role management, and compliance monitoring are necessary. Organizations should establish access review schedules, define role hierarchies, and enforce segregation of duties (SoD) policies.

4. Automate Identity Processes

Automation plays a key role in the success of an IGA implementation. Automated workflows for user provisioning, access approvals, and de-provisioning reduce manual errors and improve efficiency.

5. Conduct Regular Audits and Reviews

Continuous monitoring and periodic audits ensure that access policies remain effective. Organizations should conduct regular access reviews and use analytics to detect anomalies and potential security risks.

The Future of IGA

As technology evolves, IGA is also advancing to meet the changing landscape of cybersecurity and identity management. Emerging trends such as artificial intelligence (AI) and machine learning (ML) are being incorporated into IGA solutions to enhance threat detection, automate decision-making, and improve overall security.

Zero Trust security models, which emphasize strict identity verification and least-privilege access, are also driving changes in IGA strategies. Organizations are increasingly adopting adaptive authentication, behavior-based access controls, and real-time identity analytics to strengthen their security posture.

As businesses continue to embrace digital transformation, the importance of IGA will only grow. Organizations that prioritize identity governance and administration will be better equipped to protect sensitive data, ensure regulatory compliance, and manage identities efficiently in an ever-evolving digital world.

The Evolution of Identity Management

Identity management has come a long way from its origins as a simple method of access control to the sophisticated and automated governance solutions we see today. As organizations have grown and technology has advanced, the need for more structured and secure identity management systems has become critical. This evolution has been driven by several factors, including security concerns, regulatory compliance, and the increasing complexity of IT environments.

Early Stages: Password-Based Access Control

The earliest forms of identity management were largely manual and relied on basic authentication methods such as usernames and passwords. In the early days of computing, systems were limited to a few users, making password-based access control sufficient. Users were assigned unique credentials, and system administrators manually managed access rights. However, as organizations expanded and the number of users grew, this approach became inefficient and difficult to manage. Password reuse, weak password policies, and the lack of centralized control led to security vulnerabilities.

The Rise of Directory Services

As businesses embraced IT on a larger scale, the need for better user management became apparent. In the 1990s, directory services such as Microsoft Active Directory and LDAP (Lightweight Directory Access Protocol) emerged, offering a structured way to manage identities across an enterprise. These directory services allowed organizations to store user credentials, group memberships, and access permissions in a centralized database. This shift enabled IT teams to enforce access policies more effectively and streamline user authentication processes.

While directory services improved identity management, they still had limitations. They primarily focused on authentication and did not provide comprehensive governance capabilities. Organizations needed more robust solutions to handle provisioning, de-provisioning, and compliance requirements.

The Introduction of Identity and Access Management (IAM)

The early 2000s marked a significant shift with the introduction of Identity and Access Management (IAM) solutions. IAM expanded the scope of identity management beyond authentication and introduced features such as Single Sign-On (SSO), Multi-Factor Authentication (MFA), and role-based access control (RBAC). These features allowed organizations to enforce stricter security measures while improving user experience.

IAM systems automated user provisioning and de-provisioning, reducing the administrative burden on IT teams. Instead of manually adding and removing users from systems, IAM tools enabled organizations to define policies that automatically granted or revoked access based on predefined criteria. This automation not only improved security but also helped organizations maintain compliance with industry regulations.

The Emergence of Identity Governance and Administration (IGA)

As regulatory requirements became more stringent, organizations realized that traditional IAM solutions were not enough to address governance and compliance challenges. This led to the emergence of Identity Governance and Administration (IGA). Unlike traditional IAM, IGA focuses on the governance aspect of identity management, ensuring that access rights are granted based on business needs and regularly reviewed to prevent security risks.

IGA solutions introduced features such as access certification, policy enforcement, and audit reporting. These capabilities allowed organizations to demonstrate compliance with regulations such as GDPR, HIPAA, and SOX. By incorporating governance into identity management, organizations could mitigate the risks associated with excessive permissions and insider threats.

The Shift to Cloud-Based Identity Management

The widespread adoption of cloud computing brought new challenges and opportunities for identity management. Traditional on-premises

IAM and IGA solutions were not well-suited for cloud environments, leading to the rise of Identity-as-a-Service (IDaaS) solutions. These cloud-based identity management platforms provided organizations with scalable and flexible identity management capabilities, enabling them to secure access to both on-premises and cloud applications.

With the shift to cloud-based identity management, organizations also began adopting Zero Trust principles. Instead of assuming that users within the corporate network were trustworthy, Zero Trust required continuous authentication and verification of user identities. This approach significantly enhanced security in an era where remote work and cloud adoption became the norm.

The Role of Artificial Intelligence and Machine Learning

Modern identity management solutions have started integrating artificial intelligence (AI) and machine learning (ML) to improve security and efficiency. AI-driven identity management tools analyze user behavior, detect anomalies, and automatically adjust access permissions based on risk levels. These capabilities help organizations prevent unauthorized access and respond to security threats in real time.

Machine learning algorithms can also assist in identity lifecycle management by identifying patterns in user access requests and recommending appropriate permissions. This reduces the reliance on manual approvals and improves the overall efficiency of identity management processes.

The Future of Identity Management

Identity management will continue to evolve as technology advances and security threats become more sophisticated. The rise of decentralized identity, blockchain-based authentication, and biometric verification will play a significant role in shaping the future of identity management. Organizations will need to adopt adaptive identity management strategies that leverage AI, automation, and Zero Trust principles to stay ahead of emerging threats.

As businesses continue to digitize and regulatory requirements evolve, identity management will remain a critical component of cybersecurity and IT governance. The shift toward a more dynamic and intelligent approach to identity management will ensure that organizations can protect sensitive data, prevent unauthorized access, and maintain compliance in an increasingly complex digital landscape.

Key Concepts and Terminology in IGA

Identity Governance and Administration (IGA) is a comprehensive framework that combines identity lifecycle management with access control and compliance enforcement. Understanding the key concepts and terminology within IGA is essential for organizations aiming to implement effective identity and access management strategies. This chapter explores the foundational terms and principles that define IGA, providing clarity on how they interact within enterprise environments.

Identity and Access Management (IAM) vs. IGA

IAM is often confused with IGA, but the two serve distinct purposes. IAM refers broadly to the policies and technologies that manage digital identities and control access to systems and data. IGA, on the other hand, extends IAM by adding governance, compliance, and audit capabilities, ensuring that identity-related decisions align with security policies and regulatory requirements. While IAM focuses on authentication and authorization, IGA provides oversight, visibility, and enforcement of identity policies.

Identity Lifecycle Management

Identity lifecycle management refers to the processes involved in creating, maintaining, and retiring digital identities. This lifecycle includes:

- **Provisioning:** The creation of user accounts and assignment of access rights when a new employee, contractor, or partner joins an organization.
- **Modification:** Updates to access privileges when an individual's role changes within the organization.
- **De-provisioning:** The removal of access when an individual leaves the organization, reducing the risk of orphan accounts that could be exploited.

Automating identity lifecycle management is a core function of IGA, ensuring that access is granted and revoked in a timely and compliant manner.

Role-Based Access Control (RBAC)

RBAC is a widely used access control model that assigns permissions based on predefined roles within an organization. Instead of granting access to individuals on a case-by-case basis, RBAC structures access around job functions. This reduces administrative overhead, improves security, and ensures consistency in access provisioning.

For example, a financial analyst may require access to financial reporting systems, but not HR databases. By assigning employees to roles with predefined access privileges, organizations can streamline identity management and enforce least-privilege access.

Attribute-Based Access Control (ABAC)

ABAC extends RBAC by incorporating dynamic attributes to determine access permissions. These attributes can include user characteristics such as department, location, or security clearance, as well as contextual factors like time of access and device type. ABAC provides more granular and flexible access control than RBAC, making it ideal for organizations with complex access requirements.

Access Certification and Attestation

Access certification, also known as attestation, is the process of periodically reviewing user access to ensure it remains appropriate. Organizations conduct access reviews to verify that employees, contractors, and third parties have only the necessary permissions required for their roles. Access certification helps prevent privilege creep, where users accumulate excessive permissions over time, increasing security risks.

IGA solutions automate access certification by sending review requests to managers or compliance officers, ensuring continuous governance without manual intervention.

Segregation of Duties (SoD)

SoD is a security principle that prevents conflicts of interest and reduces fraud risk by ensuring that no single individual has excessive control over critical business processes. In IGA, SoD policies define incompatible access rights to prevent unauthorized activities.

For example, in a financial system, the same user should not have permissions to both create and approve transactions. IGA tools enforce SoD rules by detecting and preventing conflicting access assignments.

Privileged Access Management (PAM) Integration

IGA often integrates with PAM solutions to manage privileged accounts, which have elevated access rights to critical systems. Privileged accounts, such as system administrators or database administrators, pose higher security risks if compromised.

By incorporating PAM into IGA, organizations can enforce stricter controls on privileged access, such as session recording, temporary privilege escalation, and multi-factor authentication. This ensures that highly sensitive accounts are managed with enhanced security measures.

Identity Analytics and Risk-Based Access

Modern IGA solutions leverage identity analytics and risk-based access to enhance security. Identity analytics use machine learning and behavioral analysis to detect anomalies in user access patterns.

Risk-based access evaluates factors such as login location, device type, and historical behavior to determine whether access should be granted, denied, or require additional verification. By integrating these intelligent capabilities, IGA systems improve threat detection and reduce unauthorized access incidents.

Self-Service Access Requests

Self-service access requests allow users to request access to applications and resources through an automated workflow. This feature enhances efficiency by reducing the burden on IT teams while ensuring that access requests undergo proper approval processes.

Users submit access requests, which are then routed for manager approval based on predefined workflows. Once approved, IGA systems automatically provision access, reducing delays and administrative workload.

Compliance and Audit Reporting

IGA plays a crucial role in regulatory compliance by generating audit trails and compliance reports. Organizations must demonstrate adherence to security policies and regulations such as GDPR, SOX, and HIPAA.

IGA solutions provide built-in reporting features that document identity-related activities, access changes, and policy enforcement. These reports help organizations prepare for audits and ensure accountability in identity management practices.

The Future of IGA Terminology and Concepts

As organizations continue to adopt cloud technologies and zero-trust security models, IGA concepts will continue to evolve. Emerging trends such as decentralized identity, passwordless authentication, and AI-driven access management will reshape how enterprises approach identity governance.

Understanding these key concepts and terminology ensures that organizations can effectively implement IGA, strengthen security, and maintain compliance in an increasingly complex digital landscape.

The Role of IGA in Modern Enterprises

Identity Governance and Administration (IGA) plays a crucial role in modern enterprises by ensuring that users have appropriate access to corporate resources while maintaining security, compliance, and operational efficiency. As organizations expand their digital footprint, managing identities and access rights has become more complex. IGA provides a structured framework for governing digital identities, automating access management, and enforcing policies that align with business objectives and regulatory requirements.

Enhancing Security and Reducing Risk

One of the primary functions of IGA in modern enterprises is to enhance security by minimizing the risk of unauthorized access. Cyber threats continue to evolve, and attackers often exploit weak identity management practices to gain access to sensitive data. A robust IGA framework mitigates these risks by enforcing strict access controls, implementing least-privilege principles, and continuously monitoring user activities.

With automated provisioning and de-provisioning, IGA ensures that employees, contractors, and third-party users only have access to the resources necessary for their job functions. When an employee leaves the organization or changes roles, their access rights are updated or revoked in real time, reducing the risk of orphaned accounts and potential security breaches.

Furthermore, IGA solutions integrate with security information and event management (SIEM) systems to detect anomalies and suspicious access patterns. If an unauthorized access attempt is detected, automated workflows can trigger alerts or revoke access immediately, preventing potential security incidents.

Supporting Regulatory Compliance

Enterprises must comply with an increasing number of regulations and industry standards that mandate strict identity and access management controls. Regulations such as the General Data Protection Regulation (GDPR), the Sarbanes-Oxley Act (SOX), the Health Insurance Portability and Accountability Act (HIPAA), and the Payment Card Industry Data Security Standard (PCI DSS) require organizations to enforce identity governance policies and maintain audit trails of user activities.

IGA solutions help organizations meet these compliance requirements by providing features such as access certification, policy enforcement, and detailed reporting. Through automated access reviews, enterprises can ensure that only authorized personnel have access to sensitive data, reducing the risk of non-compliance.

Additionally, auditors can leverage IGA platforms to generate real-time reports that demonstrate compliance with regulatory requirements. These reports provide visibility into who accessed what resources, when, and why, making it easier for organizations to respond to audit requests and avoid potential fines or legal consequences.

Improving Operational Efficiency

Manual identity management processes can be time-consuming and prone to human error, leading to inefficiencies that impact business productivity. IGA streamlines identity and access management by automating key tasks such as user provisioning, role management, and access request approvals. This reduces the administrative burden on IT teams and enables employees to gain access to necessary resources faster.

Self-service capabilities within IGA solutions further improve efficiency by allowing users to request access to applications and data through an automated approval workflow. Instead of relying on manual intervention from IT administrators, access requests are processed based on predefined policies, reducing delays and improving user experience.

Moreover, role-based access control (RBAC) and policy-based access control (PBAC) frameworks help organizations standardize access management, ensuring that employees receive appropriate permissions based on their job roles. This prevents excessive privilege assignments and enhances overall governance.

Enabling Digital Transformation

Modern enterprises are embracing digital transformation by adopting cloud computing, remote work, and hybrid IT environments. However, these advancements also introduce new identity management challenges. Employees and contractors need secure access to cloud applications, data centers, and on-premises systems from multiple devices and locations. Without a strong IGA strategy, organizations struggle to maintain visibility and control over these distributed identities.

IGA solutions support digital transformation by providing centralized identity governance across hybrid and multi-cloud environments. Enterprises can enforce consistent access policies across all platforms, ensuring that users have seamless yet secure access to corporate resources.

Additionally, IGA enhances agility by integrating with Identity-as-a-Service (IDaaS) solutions, which provide cloud-based identity management capabilities. This allows businesses to scale their identity governance efforts as they expand into new markets or adopt new technologies.

Strengthening Identity Lifecycle Management

The role of IGA extends beyond initial access provisioning to the entire identity lifecycle. From onboarding new employees to managing role changes and terminating access when necessary, IGA ensures that identity-related processes remain accurate and up to date.

Lifecycle management automation reduces errors associated with manual updates and improves security by eliminating unnecessary access rights. By integrating with human resources (HR) systems, IGA platforms can synchronize identity data with employment status, automatically updating access permissions based on role changes or employment termination.

This level of automation not only reduces administrative overhead but also ensures compliance with security policies and regulatory requirements.

Adapting to Emerging Security Trends

As cyber threats become more sophisticated, enterprises must adopt advanced identity governance strategies to stay ahead of potential risks. IGA is evolving to incorporate artificial intelligence (AI) and machine learning (ML) capabilities, enabling organizations to detect anomalies, identify access patterns, and make data-driven decisions regarding identity governance.

Behavior-based analytics allow enterprises to detect insider threats and unusual user activity in real time. If an employee suddenly accesses sensitive data outside of their normal behavior patterns, AI-powered IGA solutions can flag the activity for review or enforce additional authentication measures.

Additionally, Zero Trust security models, which emphasize continuous verification and least-privilege access, are becoming a standard for modern enterprises. IGA plays a critical role in Zero Trust by enforcing granular access controls, verifying identities at every access point, and ensuring that only authorized users can interact with sensitive assets.

The Growing Importance of IGA in Enterprise Security

As businesses continue to evolve, so do their identity management needs. IGA has become an essential component of enterprise security, ensuring that organizations can manage identities effectively while maintaining compliance and operational efficiency. By implementing a strong IGA framework, enterprises can safeguard their digital assets, reduce security risks, and support their long-term business objectives.

IGA vs. IAM: Understanding the Difference

Identity security is a critical aspect of modern cybersecurity frameworks, ensuring that only authorized individuals can access enterprise systems and data. Within this domain, two key concepts often come into discussion: Identity and Access Management (IAM) and Identity Governance and Administration (IGA). While these terms are sometimes used interchangeably, they serve distinct purposes. Understanding the differences between IAM and IGA is essential for organizations aiming to establish a secure and compliant identity management framework.

Defining IAM and IGA

IAM is a broad discipline that encompasses all aspects of managing digital identities, authentication, and authorization. It provides mechanisms to ensure that users can access the systems, applications, and resources they need while preventing unauthorized access. IAM solutions include authentication methods such as passwords, biometrics, and multi-factor authentication (MFA), as well as authorization policies that define what users can do once inside a system.

IGA, on the other hand, extends IAM by introducing governance, oversight, and compliance into identity management. While IAM focuses on enabling and securing access, IGA ensures that access is appropriate, monitored, and aligned with business policies and regulatory requirements. IGA solutions enforce access controls, automate identity lifecycle management, and provide auditing and reporting capabilities to demonstrate compliance with standards such as GDPR, HIPAA, and SOX.

Key Differences Between IAM and IGA

One of the primary distinctions between IAM and IGA lies in their core objectives. IAM is designed to authenticate and authorize users efficiently, ensuring secure and streamlined access to digital resources. It provides immediate access control mechanisms such as Single Sign-On (SSO) and MFA to enhance security without disrupting user experience.

IGA, however, is centered around governance and administration. It focuses on answering critical questions such as: Who should have access? Why do they need access? How is access being used? By implementing access review processes, policy enforcement, and automated workflows, IGA ensures that identity-related decisions are auditable, justified, and compliant with organizational and regulatory requirements.

Authentication and Access Control vs. Identity Governance

IAM solutions emphasize authentication and access control mechanisms to verify user identities and determine their permissions. Authentication methods include password-based logins, biometric verification, and hardware tokens, while access control policies define what authenticated users can do within an application or system.

IGA introduces an additional layer of oversight by continuously evaluating and governing access rights. It ensures that users only retain necessary permissions and that access is reviewed periodically. Through role-based access control (RBAC), attribute-based access control (ABAC), and segregation of duties (SoD), IGA minimizes risks associated with excessive privileges and unauthorized access.

Identity Lifecycle Management

IAM primarily focuses on granting and enforcing access, whereas IGA takes a holistic approach to managing identity lifecycles. Identity lifecycle management in IGA includes:

- **User Onboarding and Provisioning:** Automating the creation of user accounts and assigning initial access rights based on job roles.

- **Role and Access Changes:** Adjusting permissions as users transition between roles, departments, or projects.
- **User Offboarding and De-provisioning:** Ensuring that access rights are promptly revoked when users leave the organization, reducing the risk of orphaned accounts.

By integrating lifecycle management, IGA enhances security and reduces administrative overhead, ensuring that users have the right level of access at all times.

Compliance and Auditing

A key driver for IGA adoption is regulatory compliance. Organizations must adhere to various industry regulations that mandate strict controls over user access to sensitive data. While IAM secures access through authentication and authorization, it does not inherently provide the reporting and compliance features required for audits.

IGA solutions address this gap by generating detailed audit logs, automating access certifications, and enforcing governance policies. These capabilities help organizations demonstrate compliance with regulatory mandates, mitigate security risks, and reduce the likelihood of data breaches.

Integration with Privileged Access Management (PAM)

Privileged Access Management (PAM) is another critical aspect of identity security, focusing on protecting accounts with elevated privileges. While IAM provides authentication mechanisms for privileged users, it does not inherently govern how privileged access is granted or monitored.

IGA solutions integrate with PAM to enforce governance over privileged accounts, ensuring that high-risk access is properly justified, assigned based on least privilege principles, and reviewed regularly. This integration enhances security by preventing unauthorized administrative access and reducing the risk of insider threats.

Use Cases for IAM and IGA

IAM is essential for enabling secure access in everyday business operations. It is used for:

- Implementing Single Sign-On (SSO) to simplify authentication across multiple applications.
- Enforcing Multi-Factor Authentication (MFA) to strengthen login security.
- Defining access control policies to restrict unauthorized access to sensitive systems.

IGA is necessary when organizations require additional governance and compliance measures. Common use cases include:

- Conducting periodic access reviews to verify that permissions are still appropriate.
- Automating user provisioning and de-provisioning to align with HR processes.
- Enforcing Segregation of Duties (SoD) policies to prevent fraud and conflicts of interest.

Choosing the Right Approach

Organizations must evaluate their identity security requirements to determine whether IAM, IGA, or a combination of both is necessary. In many cases, IAM and IGA work together as complementary solutions. While IAM establishes the technical controls for authentication and access enforcement, IGA provides governance, oversight, and compliance monitoring.

For organizations operating in highly regulated industries, IGA is crucial to maintaining compliance and reducing security risks. Enterprises with complex identity management needs, such as managing large workforces, third-party access, and cloud environments, benefit from IGA's automated workflows and audit capabilities.

On the other hand, businesses looking to enhance user authentication, implement SSO, or deploy MFA solutions will rely on IAM as their primary access management framework. Combining IAM with IGA ensures a comprehensive approach to identity security, balancing seamless user access with strong governance and compliance measures.

The Future of IAM and IGA

As cyber threats evolve and regulatory pressures increase, IAM and IGA will continue to play vital roles in enterprise security strategies. Emerging trends such as artificial intelligence (AI)-driven identity analytics, Zero Trust security models, and decentralized identity management will further shape the identity security landscape.

Organizations adopting modern IAM and IGA solutions will gain greater visibility into user access, reduce security risks, and streamline compliance efforts. By understanding the distinct roles of IAM and IGA, businesses can implement a robust identity security framework that meets both operational and regulatory needs.

Benefits of Implementing IGA

Identity Governance and Administration (IGA) is a critical component of modern cybersecurity strategies, helping organizations manage digital identities, enforce access policies, and ensure regulatory compliance. As enterprises grow and their IT environments become more complex, the need for a robust identity governance framework becomes essential. Implementing IGA provides numerous benefits, from strengthening security and reducing risks to enhancing operational efficiency and improving user experience.

Strengthening Security and Reducing Risk

One of the primary benefits of implementing IGA is the ability to enhance security by preventing unauthorized access to sensitive systems and data. Organizations often struggle with excessive access privileges, orphaned accounts, and privilege creep, all of which pose significant security risks. IGA solutions mitigate these risks by enforcing least-privilege access, automating identity lifecycle management, and continuously monitoring user access.

With an IGA framework in place, organizations can ensure that users only have access to the resources they need for their roles. When an employee changes positions or leaves the company, automated de-provisioning removes their access promptly, reducing the risk of insider threats. Additionally, continuous auditing and access certification processes help detect and remediate security vulnerabilities before they can be exploited.

Ensuring Regulatory Compliance

Many industries are subject to stringent regulations that require organizations to implement strict identity and access controls. Laws such as the General Data Protection Regulation (GDPR), the Sarbanes-Oxley Act (SOX), and the Health Insurance Portability and Accountability Act (HIPAA) mandate that businesses monitor, control, and report access to sensitive data.

Implementing IGA simplifies compliance by providing automated access reviews, policy enforcement, and detailed reporting capabilities. Organizations can generate audit-ready reports that demonstrate compliance with access control policies, reducing the likelihood of regulatory penalties. IGA solutions also help enforce segregation of duties (SoD) policies, preventing conflicts of interest that could lead to fraud or data breaches.

Increasing Operational Efficiency

Manually managing user identities and access rights can be time-consuming and error-prone. IT teams often spend excessive amounts of time provisioning and de-provisioning accounts, responding to access requests, and conducting access reviews. By automating these processes, IGA significantly reduces administrative overhead and improves efficiency.

Self-service access requests allow employees to request access to applications and resources through a centralized portal, reducing dependency on IT administrators. Automated approval workflows ensure that access requests are reviewed and granted based on predefined policies, eliminating delays and improving productivity. Additionally, role-based access control (RBAC) and policy-based access control (PBAC) simplify access management by grouping users with similar job functions and assigning them appropriate permissions.

Improving User Experience

A well-implemented IGA solution enhances the user experience by providing seamless and secure access to the resources employees need. Traditional access request processes often involve multiple layers of approval and manual intervention, leading to delays and frustration. With IGA, access management becomes more streamlined, enabling employees to be productive from day one.

Single Sign-On (SSO) integration within IGA solutions reduces the need for users to remember multiple passwords, minimizing password-related support requests. Additionally, self-service capabilities empower users to manage their own access, reducing the burden on IT help desks. These enhancements lead to a more efficient and user-friendly work environment.

Supporting Digital Transformation

As organizations embrace cloud computing, remote work, and hybrid IT environments, managing identities across multiple platforms becomes increasingly complex. IGA solutions provide centralized identity governance, allowing enterprises to enforce consistent access policies across on-premises and cloud applications.

By integrating with cloud-based Identity-as-a-Service (IDaaS) solutions, IGA enables organizations to extend their governance capabilities to software-as-a-service (SaaS) applications, infrastructure-as-a-service (IaaS) platforms, and other digital services. This ensures that security policies remain intact, regardless of where applications and data are hosted.

Enhancing Visibility and Control

One of the key challenges in identity management is maintaining visibility into who has access to what resources. IGA solutions provide a comprehensive view of all identities, access permissions, and entitlements across the organization. This centralized visibility helps security teams identify excessive privileges, detect policy violations, and enforce compliance requirements more effectively.

Real-time monitoring and identity analytics further enhance control by identifying unusual access patterns and potential security threats. Advanced IGA platforms leverage artificial intelligence (AI) and machine learning (ML) to detect anomalies and provide risk-based recommendations for access decisions. This proactive approach strengthens security posture and enables organizations to respond swiftly to potential threats.

Enabling Business Agility

Modern businesses require agility to adapt to changing market conditions, regulatory landscapes, and technological advancements. IGA enables enterprises to scale their identity governance efforts efficiently, whether they are onboarding new employees, expanding into new markets, or integrating new technologies.

By automating identity lifecycle management, organizations can onboard and offboard employees, contractors, and partners quickly and securely. This flexibility supports business growth while maintaining strong security and compliance standards.

Reducing Costs and Resource Demands

Implementing IGA can lead to significant cost savings by reducing manual identity management efforts, minimizing security incidents, and avoiding regulatory fines. Automating identity governance reduces the time and resources required for access certification, user provisioning, and compliance audits. Additionally, by preventing unauthorized access and reducing security risks, organizations can avoid costly data breaches and legal consequences.

IGA solutions also help optimize IT resource allocation by providing better control over software licenses, cloud service subscriptions, and application usage. By ensuring that only authorized users have access to specific resources, organizations can prevent unnecessary expenses related to unused or underutilized accounts.

Future-Proofing Identity Governance

As cybersecurity threats evolve and regulatory requirements become more stringent, organizations must continuously improve their identity governance strategies. Implementing IGA provides a future-proof foundation for managing digital identities, enabling enterprises to adapt to emerging security challenges and technological advancements.

With the integration of AI, machine learning, and behavior-based access controls, IGA is becoming more intelligent and proactive. Organizations that invest in IGA today will be better positioned to manage identities securely and efficiently in the years to come.

By implementing a comprehensive IGA framework, enterprises can enhance security, streamline operations, ensure compliance, and improve overall business agility. These benefits make IGA an essential component of any modern organization's identity and access management strategy.

Common Challenges in Identity Governance

Identity Governance and Administration (IGA) plays a critical role in managing user identities, ensuring security, and maintaining compliance with regulatory requirements. However, implementing and maintaining an effective IGA strategy is not without challenges. Organizations face numerous obstacles, ranging from technical complexities to compliance burdens and user resistance. Understanding these challenges is key to developing a robust identity governance framework that minimizes risks and enhances operational efficiency.

Complexity of Managing Diverse User Identities

One of the biggest challenges in identity governance is managing a diverse range of user identities. Organizations often have multiple user categories, including employees, contractors, third-party vendors, and business partners. Each of these groups requires different levels of access based on their roles, job functions, and the systems they need to interact with.

As businesses grow, user identities spread across various platforms, including on-premises environments, cloud services, and hybrid infrastructures. Managing identities consistently across multiple systems is a daunting task, particularly when users require access to both legacy and modern cloud-based applications. Without a centralized governance framework, organizations struggle to enforce access policies uniformly, leading to security gaps and compliance risks.

Inconsistent Role and Access Management

Role-based access control (RBAC) is a widely used approach to identity governance, but defining and maintaining roles across an enterprise can be challenging. Over time, role definitions become complex due to role proliferation, where organizations create too many roles to accommodate individual access needs. This leads to inefficiencies and difficulty in managing user permissions effectively.

Another issue is privilege creep, where users accumulate excessive access rights as they change roles within an organization. Without regular access reviews and proper de-provisioning mechanisms, employees may retain privileges they no longer need, increasing security risks. Managing role hierarchies and ensuring users only have the necessary permissions for their job functions requires continuous oversight and governance.

Compliance and Regulatory Burdens

Regulatory compliance is a driving factor behind identity governance, but meeting compliance requirements presents significant challenges. Organizations must comply with various regulations such as the General Data Protection Regulation (GDPR), the Health Insurance Portability and Accountability Act (HIPAA), the Sarbanes-Oxley Act (SOX), and industry-specific standards like the Payment Card Industry Data Security Standard (PCI DSS).

These regulations require strict access controls, audit trails, and regular certification of user privileges. However, ensuring continuous compliance across an enterprise is resource-intensive. Organizations must conduct frequent access reviews, generate compliance reports, and maintain detailed logs of identity-related activities. The complexity of compliance increases when businesses operate in multiple regions with different regulatory frameworks, requiring adaptable governance policies that can meet varying legal requirements.

Lack of Automation in Identity Lifecycle Management

Manual identity management processes are inefficient and prone to human error. Many organizations still rely on outdated, labor-intensive methods for user provisioning, access certification, and de-provisioning. This leads to delays in granting or revoking access, increasing security risks and affecting user productivity.

For instance, when an employee joins a company, IT teams must manually create accounts, assign roles, and configure permissions across multiple applications. If this process is not automated, new hires may face delays in accessing critical systems, leading to productivity losses. Similarly, when an employee leaves an organization, failing to promptly revoke access can result in orphaned accounts, which become a target for malicious exploitation.

Automation plays a key role in streamlining identity lifecycle management, ensuring that access rights are assigned and removed in a timely manner. However, implementing automation requires organizations to integrate identity governance solutions with various applications and IT infrastructure, which can be technically complex.

Managing Privileged Access and Insider Threats

Privileged accounts, such as system administrators, IT support staff, and executives, have elevated access to critical systems and data. If these accounts are not properly governed, they pose a significant security risk. Insider threats, whether intentional or accidental, can lead to data breaches, unauthorized modifications, or compliance violations.

One of the challenges organizations face is monitoring and controlling privileged access effectively. Traditional identity governance solutions often focus on standard user accounts, while privileged access management (PAM) is handled separately. Without proper integration between IGA and PAM, organizations may struggle to enforce least-privilege principles, track privileged sessions, and prevent abuse of administrative privileges.

Resistance to Change and Lack of User Awareness

Effective identity governance requires cooperation from employees, managers, and IT teams. However, organizations often face resistance when implementing new governance policies or identity management solutions. Employees may perceive additional security measures, such as multi-factor authentication (MFA) and strict access reviews, as an inconvenience rather than a necessity.

Additionally, lack of awareness about identity governance best practices leads to poor security hygiene. Users may share credentials, bypass security controls, or fail to report suspicious activities. Organizations must invest in training programs and awareness campaigns to educate employees about the importance of identity governance and their role in maintaining security.

Challenges in Integrating IGA with Existing IT Infrastructure

Many enterprises operate in complex IT environments with a mix of legacy systems, on-premises applications, and cloud-based services. Integrating IGA solutions with these disparate systems presents technical and operational challenges. Some legacy applications lack modern identity management capabilities, making it difficult to enforce centralized governance policies.

Furthermore, organizations that have undergone mergers and acquisitions may inherit multiple identity management systems, each with different policies and configurations. Consolidating these systems into a unified IGA framework requires significant effort, including data migration, policy harmonization, and system integration.

Identity Governance in a Cloud and Hybrid Environment

As organizations migrate to cloud environments, identity governance becomes more challenging. Traditional IGA solutions were designed for on-premises environments, and adapting them to cloud-based applications requires new strategies. Cloud applications often have different authentication and authorization mechanisms, making it difficult to enforce consistent access policies across all platforms.

Additionally, organizations must manage external identities, such as business partners and third-party vendors, who require access to corporate resources. Ensuring that these external identities are governed with the same level of oversight as internal employees is a growing concern. Without proper governance, businesses may expose sensitive data to unauthorized third parties.

Addressing Identity Governance Challenges

Overcoming these challenges requires a strategic approach to identity governance. Organizations must adopt modern IGA solutions that offer automation, role management, and compliance reporting. Implementing AI-driven identity analytics can help detect anomalies, identify security risks, and improve decision-making.

A strong governance framework should also include periodic access reviews, integration with privileged access management, and continuous monitoring of user activities. Organizations must prioritize user training and change management initiatives to ensure that employees understand and comply with identity governance policies.

As the digital landscape continues to evolve, businesses must remain proactive in addressing identity governance challenges. A well-defined IGA strategy enhances security, reduces compliance risks, and improves operational efficiency, allowing organizations to manage identities effectively in an increasingly complex IT environment.

Developing an IGA Strategy

Identity Governance and Administration (IGA) is essential for modern enterprises to ensure secure, efficient, and compliant management of digital identities. A well-developed IGA strategy enables organizations to control user access, enforce policies, and maintain oversight over identity-related risks. Implementing IGA requires careful planning, alignment with business objectives, and continuous improvement to adapt to evolving security threats and regulatory requirements.

Understanding the Need for an IGA Strategy

Organizations today operate in complex IT environments that include on-premises systems, cloud applications, and hybrid infrastructures. Managing user identities across these diverse platforms presents challenges, particularly as the workforce becomes more mobile and includes contractors, third-party vendors, and remote employees. Without a structured IGA strategy, organizations face risks such as unauthorized access, privilege creep, compliance violations, and security breaches.

A well-defined IGA strategy helps organizations mitigate these risks by providing a framework for identity lifecycle management, access controls, and governance policies. By integrating automation and analytics, enterprises can improve efficiency, enhance security, and reduce administrative overhead associated with identity management.

Establishing Business Objectives and Compliance Requirements

The first step in developing an IGA strategy is identifying business objectives and regulatory requirements. Every organization has unique security and governance needs based on industry standards, data protection laws, and operational priorities. Companies in highly regulated industries, such as finance and healthcare, must adhere to stringent compliance mandates, including GDPR, HIPAA, and SOX.

Aligning IGA with business goals ensures that identity management processes support operational efficiency without compromising security. This involves defining key performance indicators (KPIs) to measure the effectiveness of identity governance efforts. Common KPIs include time to provision and de-provision accounts, percentage of orphaned accounts eliminated, and compliance audit success rates.

Defining Identity Governance Policies

An effective IGA strategy requires well-defined policies governing user access, role assignments, and security measures. Organizations must establish clear guidelines on who can access specific systems, how access requests are handled, and how frequently access reviews are conducted.

Policies should cover:

- **Role-Based Access Control (RBAC):** Defining job-based access privileges to minimize excessive permissions.
- **Segregation of Duties (SoD):** Preventing conflicts of interest by restricting users from having conflicting permissions, such as the ability to both initiate and approve financial transactions.
- **Access Certification:** Conducting periodic reviews to ensure access remains appropriate and necessary.

Establishing governance policies early in the strategy development process ensures consistency in access control and compliance enforcement.

Implementing Automation for Identity Lifecycle Management

Manual identity management processes are inefficient and error-prone. Automating user provisioning, role assignments, and de-provisioning improves accuracy and reduces administrative workload. A well-implemented IGA strategy leverages automation to:

- **Provision new users based on job roles and department policies.**
- **Modify access rights automatically when employees change roles.**
- **Revoke access immediately when employees leave the organization.**

Automation also enhances compliance by generating audit logs and enforcing policies consistently across all identity-related processes. Integrating IGA solutions with HR systems ensures seamless updates when employees join, move within, or exit an organization.

Integrating IGA with Existing IT Infrastructure

Successful IGA implementation depends on seamless integration with enterprise IT infrastructure, including identity providers, cloud platforms, and privileged access management (PAM) solutions. Organizations must evaluate their current technology landscape and select an IGA platform that supports interoperability with existing tools.

Key integration points include:

- **Single Sign-On (SSO) and Multi-Factor Authentication (MFA):** Enhancing security while providing a frictionless user experience.
- **Cloud and On-Premises Applications:** Managing access to both legacy systems and modern SaaS applications.
- **Security Information and Event Management (SIEM) Systems:** Enabling real-time monitoring and threat detection based on identity analytics.

By ensuring that IGA solutions work in harmony with other security technologies, organizations can maximize the effectiveness of their identity governance strategy.

Conducting Regular Access Reviews and Audits

IGA strategies must include mechanisms for continuous monitoring, access reviews, and compliance audits. Regular audits help organizations identify security gaps, detect orphaned accounts, and prevent privilege creep.

Access reviews involve managers and system owners verifying whether users still require access to specific applications and data. Automating these reviews through IGA solutions reduces manual effort and ensures compliance with regulatory requirements. Organizations should also implement risk-based access monitoring to detect anomalies and unauthorized access attempts.

Educating Users and Encouraging Compliance

Successful IGA strategies require user awareness and participation. Employees, managers, and IT administrators must understand the importance of identity governance and follow established policies. Organizations should invest in security awareness training to:

- Educate employees on secure password management and phishing threats.
- Train managers on how to conduct access reviews effectively.
- Provide IT teams with knowledge of IGA best practices and policy enforcement.

By fostering a culture of security and compliance, organizations can ensure that identity governance remains a shared responsibility across all departments.

Adapting to Evolving Security Threats and Business Needs

Identity governance is not a one-time project but an ongoing process that must evolve with changing security landscapes and business priorities. Organizations must stay ahead of emerging threats, such as insider attacks and credential-based cyberattacks, by continuously refining their IGA strategy.

Artificial intelligence (AI) and machine learning (ML) are becoming increasingly important in identity governance, allowing organizations to analyze user behavior, detect anomalies, and automate risk-based access decisions. Implementing AI-driven identity analytics can enhance threat detection and provide deeper insights into access patterns.

As organizations expand their digital footprint, they must also consider the role of identity governance in supporting cloud adoption, remote work, and third-party access management. An agile and adaptive IGA strategy ensures that security and compliance remain intact, even as business operations evolve.

Achieving a Balanced and Effective IGA Strategy

Developing an IGA strategy requires a balance between security, compliance, and user experience. Organizations must design a governance framework that enforces strict security controls while ensuring seamless access for authorized users.

By aligning identity governance with business goals, automating identity lifecycle processes, integrating IGA solutions with existing IT infrastructure, and continuously monitoring access, organizations can build a resilient identity governance strategy. This approach not only strengthens security but also enhances operational efficiency and regulatory compliance, ensuring long-term success in identity management.

Choosing the Right IGA Tools

Selecting the right Identity Governance and Administration (IGA) tools is a critical step in ensuring the security, compliance, and efficiency of an organization's identity management strategy. With the increasing complexity of IT environments, businesses must invest in tools that streamline identity lifecycle management, enforce access policies, and provide audit capabilities. The choice of an IGA solution impacts not only security but also operational efficiency and regulatory adherence. Understanding key factors in evaluating IGA tools helps organizations make informed decisions that align with their business needs.

Understanding Business Requirements

Before selecting an IGA tool, organizations must assess their specific requirements. Each business has unique identity governance needs based on its size, industry, regulatory landscape, and existing IT infrastructure. Enterprises with a highly dynamic workforce, such as those relying on contractors and third-party vendors, may prioritize automated user provisioning and de-provisioning. Highly regulated industries, such as finance and healthcare, require robust compliance and audit capabilities to meet legal mandates.

Identifying key use cases ensures that the selected IGA tool supports essential business functions. For example, some organizations require deep integration with cloud platforms like Microsoft Azure, AWS, or Google Cloud, while others prioritize seamless integration with legacy on-premises applications. Understanding these needs helps filter out tools that lack critical functionalities.

Core Features to Look for in an IGA Solution

An effective IGA tool must provide a comprehensive set of features to support identity lifecycle management, access control, compliance enforcement, and security monitoring. The following capabilities are essential when evaluating IGA solutions:

Identity Lifecycle Management

Managing the full lifecycle of user identities is a fundamental function of IGA. A robust tool should automate the provisioning and de-provisioning of user accounts across various systems, ensuring that employees, contractors, and partners have appropriate access from onboarding to offboarding. Automated role-based provisioning minimizes the risk of human error and reduces administrative overhead.

Access Certification and Review

IGA solutions should support periodic access reviews to verify that users only have the necessary permissions. Automated certification campaigns allow managers and system owners to review access rights efficiently. This feature is critical for organizations that need to comply with regulations requiring regular audits of user access.

Role-Based and Policy-Based Access Control

A good IGA tool should provide both Role-Based Access Control (RBAC) and Policy-Based Access Control (PBAC). RBAC enables organizations to assign permissions based on predefined roles, reducing complexity in managing individual user access. PBAC offers greater flexibility by enforcing access policies based on attributes such as user department, location, or device type.

Integration with Existing IT Infrastructure

Seamless integration with existing applications, cloud services, and enterprise systems is crucial. The IGA tool should support standard authentication protocols like SAML, OAuth, and SCIM to facilitate smooth interoperability. Organizations with hybrid environments need solutions that work across on-premises and cloud applications without requiring extensive customization.

Self-Service Access Requests

Self-service capabilities empower users to request access to applications and data without relying on IT administrators. The tool should provide an intuitive interface for users to submit requests, while incorporating approval workflows to ensure access is granted securely. This functionality improves efficiency and reduces administrative burden.

Compliance and Audit Reporting

Regulatory compliance is a major driver for IGA adoption. The chosen tool must generate detailed reports on user access, policy enforcement, and access certifications. These reports should be audit-ready, allowing organizations to demonstrate compliance with GDPR, HIPAA, SOX, and other regulatory frameworks.

Privileged Access Management (PAM) Integration

While IGA manages standard user accounts, privileged accounts require additional oversight. Some IGA tools offer built-in privileged access management features, while others integrate with dedicated PAM solutions. Organizations with high-security needs should ensure that their IGA solution supports governance over privileged identities.

Cloud-Based vs. On-Premises IGA Solutions

Organizations must decide whether to deploy an on-premises IGA solution or adopt a cloud-based Identity-as-a-Service (IDaaS) model. Each option has distinct advantages and limitations.

- **On-Premises IGA** solutions provide full control over data and security policies, making them suitable for businesses with strict data residency requirements. However, they require significant IT resources for deployment and maintenance.
- **Cloud-Based IGA (IDaaS)** solutions offer scalability, ease of deployment, and automatic updates. These tools are ideal for organizations embracing digital transformation and cloud migration. However, businesses must evaluate data security and integration capabilities when considering IDaaS options.

Evaluating Scalability and Performance

As organizations grow, their identity governance needs evolve. A scalable IGA tool can accommodate increasing numbers of users, applications, and policies without degrading performance. Businesses should assess how well an IGA solution handles high transaction volumes, complex workflows, and future expansions. Performance testing during the evaluation phase ensures that the tool can operate efficiently in large-scale environments.

Vendor Reputation and Support Services

Choosing a reputable IGA vendor is as important as selecting the tool itself. Organizations should evaluate vendors based on their experience, customer reviews, and support offerings. Key considerations include:

- **Product roadmap and innovation:** A strong vendor continuously updates its IGA solutions to address emerging security threats and compliance requirements.
- **Customer support:** Reliable technical support and training resources are essential for smooth implementation and ongoing maintenance.
- **User community and documentation:** A well-documented solution with an active user community ensures better troubleshooting and knowledge sharing.

Total Cost of Ownership (TCO)

While cost should not be the sole determining factor, organizations must evaluate the total cost of ownership (TCO) for an IGA solution. Licensing fees, implementation costs, customization expenses, and ongoing maintenance all contribute to TCO. A solution with lower upfront costs may require extensive configuration, increasing long-term expenses. Conducting a cost-benefit analysis ensures that the selected IGA tool provides value while remaining within budget.

Proof of Concept and Pilot Testing

Before committing to a full-scale deployment, organizations should conduct a proof of concept (PoC) to test the IGA tool in their environment. A PoC allows IT teams to validate integration capabilities, evaluate performance, and assess user experience. Running a pilot program with a small user group helps identify potential challenges and refine deployment strategies before rolling out the solution organization-wide.

Making the Right Choice for Long-Term Success

Selecting the right IGA tool is a strategic decision that impacts security, compliance, and operational efficiency. Businesses must prioritize solutions that align with their current needs while providing scalability for future growth. A well-chosen IGA tool not only simplifies identity management but also enhances security posture and regulatory adherence. Investing time in thorough evaluation ensures that organizations implement a solution that supports their long-term identity governance objectives.

Building an Effective IGA Framework

Identity Governance and Administration (IGA) is a foundational component of an organization's security and compliance strategy. A well-structured IGA framework ensures that identities are managed effectively, access rights are properly assigned, and regulatory requirements are met. As organizations grow, the complexity of managing digital identities increases, making it essential to implement an IGA framework that balances security, efficiency, and compliance.

Understanding the Need for an IGA Framework

Organizations operate in an environment where digital identities extend beyond employees to include contractors, partners, and third-party vendors. With access to enterprise systems and sensitive data, these identities must be managed securely to prevent unauthorized access and data breaches. A structured IGA framework helps organizations control access, automate identity lifecycle management, and enforce security policies.

A well-designed IGA framework also supports regulatory compliance by ensuring access controls meet the requirements of frameworks such as GDPR, HIPAA, and SOX. Without a proper governance model, organizations risk audit failures, data breaches, and operational inefficiencies.

Defining Governance Policies and Access Controls

The foundation of an effective IGA framework lies in well-defined governance policies. Organizations must establish rules for identity creation, access provisioning, and role assignments. These policies should align with business objectives while maintaining security and compliance.

Key governance policies include:

- **Access Control Policies:** Defining who can access what resources based on job roles, department, and business requirements.
- **Role-Based Access Control (RBAC):** Assigning permissions based on predefined job functions to minimize excessive access.
- **Segregation of Duties (SoD):** Preventing conflicts of interest by ensuring users do not have conflicting access rights, such as the ability to initiate and approve financial transactions.
- **Access Certification:** Conducting periodic reviews to validate user access and remove unnecessary privileges.

By defining and enforcing these policies, organizations can maintain a structured approach to identity governance.

Automating Identity Lifecycle Management

Manually managing user identities and access rights is inefficient and prone to errors. Automation is a critical component of an effective IGA framework, ensuring that user access is granted and revoked promptly based on predefined policies.

Key areas of automation include:

- **User Provisioning:** Automatically creating accounts and assigning access when employees, contractors, or third-party users join an organization.
- **Role Changes:** Adjusting access privileges when employees change job functions or departments.
- **De-Provisioning:** Revoking access immediately when users leave the organization to prevent security risks.

By integrating automation into identity governance, organizations reduce administrative burdens and enhance security posture.

Implementing Strong Authentication and Authorization Mechanisms

An effective IGA framework integrates with authentication and authorization mechanisms to ensure secure access to enterprise systems. Implementing Single Sign-On (SSO) reduces the number of credentials users need while improving access security. Multi-Factor Authentication (MFA) adds an extra layer of protection by requiring multiple verification methods before granting access.

In addition to authentication, policy-based access control (PBAC) provides dynamic access management based on contextual factors such as location, device type, and risk level. This approach ensures that access decisions are made in real time, improving security without compromising user productivity.

Integrating IGA with IT and Security Infrastructure

An IGA framework must seamlessly integrate with an organization's IT and security infrastructure. Identity management tools should connect with enterprise applications, cloud platforms, and privileged access management (PAM) solutions to ensure consistent access control across all environments.

Key integrations include:

- **HR Systems:** Synchronizing identity data with employment records to automate onboarding and offboarding.
- **Cloud Platforms:** Extending governance to cloud applications and infrastructure-as-a-service (IaaS) environments.
- **Security Information and Event Management (SIEM) Systems:** Providing real-time identity monitoring and threat detection.

With proper integration, organizations gain centralized visibility into identity-related activities, reducing security gaps and improving compliance.

Conducting Regular Access Reviews and Compliance Audits

To maintain a strong IGA framework, organizations must conduct regular access reviews and compliance audits. Periodic evaluations help identify security risks, detect unauthorized access, and ensure that users only have permissions relevant to their job functions.

Access reviews should involve key stakeholders, including managers and IT administrators, to verify user access rights. Automated workflows streamline the review process, reducing the time and effort required for manual audits.

Additionally, compliance reporting tools generate detailed audit logs that demonstrate adherence to regulatory requirements. These reports help organizations prepare for external audits and avoid potential penalties for non-compliance.

Enhancing Security with Identity Analytics and AI

Advancements in artificial intelligence (AI) and identity analytics are transforming IGA frameworks. AI-driven solutions analyze user behavior, detect anomalies, and recommend access changes based on risk assessments.

Identity analytics provide insights into access trends, helping organizations optimize role definitions and eliminate excessive permissions. By incorporating machine learning algorithms, IGA solutions can identify patterns that indicate potential security threats, such as unauthorized access attempts or privilege misuse.

Addressing User Experience and Change Management

A successful IGA framework must balance security and user experience. Employees require quick access to applications and data, while IT teams must enforce strict access controls. To address these needs, organizations should implement user-friendly self-service portals for access requests and password resets.

Change management is also essential when introducing an IGA framework. Employees, managers, and IT staff must understand the importance of identity governance and their role in maintaining security. Training programs and awareness initiatives help ensure smooth adoption and compliance with identity policies.

Adapting to Evolving Business Needs

Identity governance is not a static process. As organizations grow and technology evolves, IGA frameworks must adapt to new security challenges and business requirements. The shift to cloud computing, remote work, and Zero Trust security models requires continuous refinement of identity governance strategies.

Organizations should regularly assess their IGA framework's effectiveness, update governance policies, and implement new security controls as needed. By staying proactive, businesses can maintain strong identity governance while supporting innovation and digital transformation.

Achieving a Scalable and Resilient IGA Framework

A well-structured IGA framework provides a scalable and resilient foundation for identity management. By defining governance policies, automating identity processes, integrating security tools, and leveraging AI-driven analytics, organizations can enhance security, improve compliance, and streamline access management.

As enterprises navigate an increasingly complex IT landscape, building a robust IGA framework ensures that identities remain secure, governance remains enforceable, and business operations remain efficient.

Role-Based Access Control (RBAC) and Its Importance

Role-Based Access Control (RBAC) is a widely adopted framework for managing user permissions in organizations. It is designed to ensure that users have appropriate access based on their job roles, reducing security risks and improving operational efficiency. As enterprises expand their IT environments, the need for structured and scalable access control mechanisms becomes critical. RBAC provides a systematic way to assign and manage access rights, ensuring that only authorized individuals can access sensitive systems and data.

Understanding Role-Based Access Control

RBAC operates on the principle that access to resources should be determined by a user's role within the organization. Instead of assigning permissions to individuals on a case-by-case basis, RBAC groups users based on job functions and assigns access rights accordingly. This approach simplifies identity management, reduces administrative overhead, and enhances security.

In an RBAC system, roles are predefined according to business functions. For example, an organization may have roles such as "HR Manager," "Financial Analyst," or "IT Administrator." Each role is associated with specific permissions that define what actions users can perform within applications, databases, or network systems. When a new employee joins, they are assigned a role that automatically grants them the necessary access. If they change positions, their access rights are updated to match their new responsibilities.

The Importance of RBAC in Modern Enterprises

RBAC plays a crucial role in securing enterprise systems by enforcing the principle of least privilege. Users are granted only the permissions necessary to perform their job duties, reducing the risk of unauthorized access and insider threats. Without a structured access control model, employees may accumulate excessive permissions over time, increasing the potential for security breaches.

By implementing RBAC, organizations can streamline access control processes and improve compliance with regulatory requirements. Many industries, including healthcare, finance, and government, are subject to strict data protection laws. Regulations such as the General Data Protection Regulation (GDPR), the Health Insurance Portability and Accountability Act (HIPAA), and the Sarbanes-Oxley Act (SOX) mandate that organizations enforce strict access controls. RBAC helps businesses meet these requirements by providing a clear and auditable access control framework.

Key Components of RBAC

RBAC consists of several core components that define how access permissions are assigned and enforced:

- **Roles:** A collection of access permissions associated with a specific job function. Users are assigned to roles rather than individual permissions.
- **Permissions:** The specific actions that a role can perform within a system, such as reading, writing, editing, or deleting data.
- **Users:** Individuals who are assigned roles based on their responsibilities within the organization.
- **Role Hierarchies:** A structure that defines relationships between roles, allowing higher-level roles to inherit permissions from lower-level roles.
- **Separation of Duties (SoD):** A security principle that ensures conflicting responsibilities are not assigned to a single user. For example, a user who approves financial transactions should not also have the ability to create them.

Benefits of RBAC Implementation

RBAC provides numerous advantages that improve security, efficiency, and compliance. One of the most significant benefits is **reduced administrative burden**. Instead of managing individual user permissions, IT administrators define roles and assign users to those roles. This simplifies user provisioning and de-provisioning, particularly in large organizations with high employee turnover.

Another key advantage is **enhanced security**. By limiting access to only what is necessary for each role, RBAC reduces the risk of accidental or intentional data breaches. It also helps protect against insider threats by preventing employees from accessing systems unrelated to their job functions.

RBAC also supports **regulatory compliance** by enforcing access policies that align with legal requirements. Auditors can easily review access control policies, track changes, and generate reports that demonstrate compliance with industry standards.

Challenges of Implementing RBAC

Despite its benefits, RBAC implementation can be complex, particularly for large organizations with dynamic access needs. One common challenge is **role explosion**, where an excessive number of roles are created to accommodate varying access requirements. This can lead to administrative difficulties and increased complexity in managing access rights.

To prevent role explosion, organizations should adopt a **role engineering approach**, carefully designing roles based on business processes and access needs. Conducting a thorough role analysis helps define clear and manageable roles that align with organizational structure.

Another challenge is **role maintenance**. As business processes evolve, roles and permissions must be updated to reflect changes in job responsibilities. Regular access reviews and audits help ensure that RBAC policies remain effective and up to date.

Best Practices for RBAC Implementation

Successful RBAC deployment requires careful planning and continuous management. Organizations should start by conducting a **business needs assessment** to identify key roles and the permissions required for each. Engaging stakeholders from different departments ensures that role definitions align with operational needs.

Once roles are defined, implementing **least privilege principles** ensures that users only receive the minimum permissions required to perform their tasks. Regularly reviewing and adjusting roles prevents privilege creep and minimizes security risks.

Automating RBAC processes can further improve efficiency and accuracy. Integrating RBAC with Identity Governance and

Administration (IGA) solutions allows organizations to automate user provisioning, enforce access policies, and conduct access reviews with minimal manual effort.

The Future of RBAC

As cybersecurity threats continue to evolve, RBAC is adapting to new challenges and technological advancements. The rise of **dynamic access control models**, such as Attribute-Based Access Control (ABAC) and Risk-Based Access Control, is complementing traditional RBAC by introducing more granular and adaptive access policies.

Organizations are also integrating **artificial intelligence (AI) and machine learning** into identity governance to analyze access patterns and detect anomalies. AI-driven identity analytics can help refine role definitions, identify excessive privileges, and recommend adjustments to RBAC policies.

RBAC remains a foundational component of identity and access management, providing a structured and scalable approach to access control. By implementing RBAC effectively, organizations can enhance security, improve compliance, and streamline identity management across their IT environments.

Understanding Policy-Based Access Control (PBAC)

Policy-Based Access Control (PBAC) is an advanced access control model that allows organizations to enforce security policies dynamically based on contextual attributes. Unlike traditional access control methods that rely on predefined roles or hierarchical permissions, PBAC grants access based on policies that evaluate attributes such as user identity, device type, location, risk level, and time of access. This approach provides greater flexibility and security, making it ideal for modern enterprises operating in complex IT environments.

The Evolution of Access Control

Traditional access control models such as Role-Based Access Control (RBAC) and Discretionary Access Control (DAC) have limitations in dynamic and large-scale environments. RBAC, for example, assigns permissions based on roles, but it struggles with adaptability when users require temporary or conditional access. In contrast, PBAC introduces a more adaptive approach by considering multiple factors before granting access, ensuring that security policies align with real-time conditions.

Organizations that rely solely on static roles often face challenges such as role explosion, where too many roles exist to accommodate varying levels of access. PBAC alleviates this issue by allowing policies to govern access dynamically, reducing administrative overhead and improving security compliance.

How PBAC Works

PBAC evaluates access requests based on policies defined by administrators. These policies use a set of attributes to determine whether access should be granted or denied. The core components of PBAC include:

- **Subjects:** The entities requesting access, such as users, applications, or devices.
- **Resources:** The systems, applications, or data that the subject seeks to access.
- **Actions:** The operations the subject intends to perform, such as read, write, or modify.
- **Contextual Attributes:** Additional factors that influence access decisions, such as location, time of request, device security posture, or authentication strength.

For example, an employee working from an office may have unrestricted access to a database, while the same employee attempting to access it from an untrusted device outside the corporate network may be denied or required to authenticate with multi-factor authentication (MFA).

Benefits of PBAC

PBAC provides several advantages over traditional access control models, making it a preferred choice for organizations requiring high levels of security, flexibility, and regulatory compliance.

Enhanced Security

By evaluating multiple attributes before granting access, PBAC reduces security risks associated with static role assignments. Even if a user's role permits access, additional contextual checks can restrict access if conditions indicate a potential security threat.

Granular Access Control

PBAC enables fine-grained access control by allowing administrators to define policies that consider a wide range of attributes. This ensures that users receive the minimum level of access required for their tasks, reducing the risk of privilege misuse.

Dynamic and Adaptive Policies

One of the key strengths of PBAC is its adaptability. Unlike RBAC, which requires manual updates to accommodate changes, PBAC policies automatically adjust access based on real-time conditions. This dynamic nature is particularly useful in cloud environments and Zero Trust security models, where access decisions must adapt to changing risk levels.

Regulatory Compliance

Many industries, including healthcare, finance, and government, must comply with strict regulations regarding data access and security. PBAC helps organizations enforce compliance policies by ensuring that only authorized users can access sensitive data under specific conditions. This reduces the risk of non-compliance and simplifies audit processes.

Implementing PBAC in an Organization

To successfully implement PBAC, organizations must follow a structured approach that includes policy definition, integration with existing identity systems, and continuous monitoring.

Defining Policies

Organizations should begin by identifying key access control requirements and defining policies that align with security and business objectives. Policies should be structured using logical conditions, such as:

- "Allow access to financial reports if the user is in the finance department and is accessing from a corporate-managed device."
- "Require additional authentication if the user is attempting to access sensitive data from an external network."

Clear policy definitions ensure that PBAC is effective and aligns with security best practices.

Integrating with Identity and Security Systems

PBAC requires integration with identity providers, security information and event management (SIEM) systems, and cloud access security brokers (CASBs). These integrations provide the necessary context for making informed access control decisions.

Organizations should ensure that PBAC policies work seamlessly with existing Single Sign-On (SSO), Multi-Factor Authentication (MFA), and Privileged Access Management (PAM) solutions to create a comprehensive security framework.

Continuous Monitoring and Optimization

Access control policies should be continuously monitored and refined based on security trends and business needs. Organizations can use identity analytics and artificial intelligence to detect anomalies, improve policy effectiveness, and enhance threat detection. Regular access reviews and policy audits help ensure that PBAC remains aligned with organizational security requirements.

Challenges of PBAC Adoption

While PBAC offers significant benefits, its adoption comes with challenges that organizations must address to ensure a smooth transition.

Complex Policy Management

Defining and managing PBAC policies requires a deep understanding of business processes, security risks, and contextual factors. Organizations may struggle to create policies that balance security with usability, requiring careful planning and iterative refinement.

Integration Complexity

PBAC relies on multiple data sources to evaluate access requests. Integrating PBAC with legacy systems, cloud applications, and security tools can be complex, requiring significant investment in technology and expertise.

Performance Considerations

Because PBAC evaluates multiple attributes before granting access, there is potential for increased processing time. Organizations must optimize their PBAC implementation to ensure that access decisions are made efficiently without impacting user experience.

The Future of PBAC

As organizations adopt Zero Trust security models and cloud-based architectures, PBAC will play a crucial role in shaping the future of access control. Advancements in artificial intelligence and machine learning will enhance PBAC capabilities by enabling automated policy adjustments based on evolving security threats.

Organizations seeking to strengthen their access control mechanisms should consider PBAC as a strategic investment. By adopting a policy-driven approach to identity governance, businesses can achieve a higher level of security, compliance, and operational flexibility.

Identity Lifecycle Management

Identity Lifecycle Management (ILM) is a crucial aspect of modern cybersecurity and identity governance, ensuring that user identities are created, managed, and retired in a structured and secure manner. As organizations grow and digital transformation accelerates, managing user identities across various applications, platforms, and environments becomes increasingly complex. A well-defined ILM strategy enhances security, improves operational efficiency, and ensures compliance with regulatory requirements.

Understanding Identity Lifecycle Management

ILM refers to the entire process of managing digital identities from the moment a user joins an organization to their departure. It encompasses user provisioning, role assignments, access modifications, and eventual de-provisioning. Effective ILM ensures that users have the right level of access at the right time while preventing security risks such as unauthorized access, privilege creep, and orphaned accounts.

By automating identity lifecycle processes, organizations can reduce manual effort, minimize errors, and enforce security policies consistently. This approach also helps businesses comply with industry regulations such as GDPR, HIPAA, and SOX, which mandate strict access controls and audit requirements.

Key Stages of Identity Lifecycle Management

ILM consists of several critical stages that define how user identities are managed within an organization:

1. User Onboarding and Provisioning

The identity lifecycle begins when a new user—whether an employee, contractor, or partner—joins an organization. At this stage, an identity is created in the system, and appropriate access rights are assigned based on job role, department, or predefined policies.

Automated provisioning tools streamline this process by integrating with HR systems to detect new hires and generate accounts across multiple applications. Role-based access control (RBAC) ensures that users receive only the necessary permissions for their responsibilities, reducing the risk of excessive access.

2. Role and Access Management

As users perform their duties, their access needs may change. Employees may receive promotions, switch departments, or take on additional responsibilities that require modified access rights. Without proper governance, access modifications can lead to privilege creep, where users accumulate excessive permissions over time.

ILM ensures that role-based and policy-based access controls are enforced, automatically adjusting user permissions based on predefined rules. Organizations must implement regular access reviews to verify that users retain only the necessary permissions.

3. User Self-Service and Access Requests

Modern ILM frameworks incorporate self-service capabilities that allow users to request access to applications and resources through automated approval workflows. This reduces the burden on IT teams while ensuring that access requests undergo proper validation.

Self-service access management enhances user experience by reducing wait times for approvals while maintaining compliance through multi-level approval processes and audit trails.

4. Monitoring and Auditing

Continuous monitoring of user activity and access patterns is essential for maintaining security. ILM solutions integrate with Security Information and Event Management (SIEM) systems to detect anomalies, such as unauthorized login attempts or unusual access behaviors.

Regular audits ensure compliance with internal policies and external regulations. Audit logs track identity-related events, providing visibility into access modifications, failed authentication attempts, and policy violations.

5. User Offboarding and De-Provisioning

When an employee leaves the organization or a contractor's engagement ends, access to enterprise systems must be revoked immediately. Failure to remove access in a timely manner can result in security vulnerabilities, as former employees may retain credentials that allow unauthorized access.

Automated de-provisioning ensures that all accounts associated with a departing user are disabled, reducing the risk of orphaned accounts. Additionally, organizations should implement exit reviews to confirm that no access rights persist beyond the user's tenure.

Benefits of Effective Identity Lifecycle Management

A well-implemented ILM strategy offers several advantages that enhance security, efficiency, and compliance:

- **Improved Security:** Ensures that users only have access to the resources they need, reducing the risk of unauthorized access and insider threats.

- **Regulatory Compliance:** Helps organizations adhere to legal and industry regulations by enforcing strict access controls and maintaining audit trails.
- **Operational Efficiency:** Reduces manual workload for IT administrators by automating identity provisioning, access modifications, and de-provisioning.
- **Enhanced User Experience:** Provides employees with timely access to necessary resources, improving productivity and reducing frustration.

Challenges in Implementing ILM

Despite its benefits, ILM presents challenges that organizations must address to ensure successful implementation:

- **Integration Complexity:** Connecting ILM systems with multiple applications, cloud platforms, and legacy systems can be difficult.
- **Role Management Issues:** Defining and maintaining role hierarchies can lead to role explosion, where too many roles create administrative inefficiencies.
- **Compliance Burden:** Organizations operating in multiple jurisdictions must navigate varying regulatory requirements while maintaining consistent identity policies.

To overcome these challenges, businesses must invest in scalable ILM solutions, automate routine identity tasks, and conduct regular reviews of their identity governance frameworks.

The Future of Identity Lifecycle Management

As cybersecurity threats evolve, ILM is increasingly incorporating artificial intelligence (AI) and machine learning (ML) to enhance security. AI-driven identity analytics help detect anomalies, predict access needs, and automate risk-based decision-making.

The rise of Zero Trust security models also influences ILM, requiring continuous verification of user identities rather than relying solely on initial authentication. Future ILM solutions will focus on adaptive authentication, real-time risk analysis, and increased automation to meet the demands of dynamic enterprise environments.

Organizations that invest in robust ILM strategies will be better equipped to manage digital identities securely, maintain regulatory compliance, and improve operational efficiency in an increasingly complex IT landscape.

Automating User Provisioning and De-provisioning

User provisioning and de-provisioning are essential aspects of identity governance, ensuring that users receive the right level of access to enterprise resources when they join an organization and have their access promptly revoked when they leave. Manual processes for managing user accounts are inefficient, error-prone, and can expose organizations to security risks. Automating provisioning and de-provisioning streamlines access management, enhances security, and ensures compliance with regulatory requirements.

The Importance of Automating User Provisioning

User provisioning is the process of creating and managing digital identities within an organization. It involves granting access to systems, applications, and data based on a user's role, department, or job function. Traditional manual provisioning often leads to delays, misconfigurations, and inconsistencies in access assignments, which can impact productivity and security.

Automation eliminates these challenges by ensuring that new employees, contractors, and third-party vendors receive appropriate access immediately upon onboarding. When integrated with human resources (HR) systems, automated provisioning solutions can synchronize identity attributes, ensuring that access is granted based on predefined policies.

By implementing automated workflows, organizations can reduce dependency on IT administrators and speed up the onboarding process. Employees can start working immediately with the necessary permissions, improving efficiency while reducing the risk of human error in access assignments.

Enhancing Security Through Automated De-provisioning

While provisioning ensures that users receive the right access, de-provisioning is equally critical in maintaining security. Failure to promptly remove access when employees leave the company or change roles can result in orphaned accounts—active credentials that remain linked to former employees. These accounts become prime targets for cybercriminals and insider threats.

Automated de-provisioning eliminates this risk by revoking access in real-time when an employee departs. By integrating with HR and directory services, automated de-provisioning ensures that when a termination is recorded, associated access privileges are immediately revoked across all systems.

Another key aspect of de-provisioning is access revocation for users who change roles within the organization. Employees moving from one department to another may require different permissions, and old access rights should be removed to prevent privilege creep. Automation ensures that users maintain only the access necessary for their new roles, reducing security risks and enforcing the principle of least privilege.

Integration with Identity Governance and Administration (IGA) Systems

Automated provisioning and de-provisioning are most effective when integrated with Identity Governance and Administration (IGA) solutions. These platforms provide centralized identity lifecycle management, enforcing governance policies and ensuring compliance.

IGA solutions enable organizations to:

- Define role-based and policy-based access controls to automate access assignments.
- Implement approval workflows for high-risk access requests.
- Conduct periodic access reviews to validate user permissions.
- Maintain audit logs of provisioning and de-provisioning actions for compliance reporting.

With an IGA framework, automation is governed by strict policies that ensure consistent and auditable identity management processes.

Reducing Administrative Overhead and Improving Efficiency

Manual user provisioning and de-provisioning require IT teams to handle access requests, process approvals, and manage account updates, consuming valuable time and resources. Automating these tasks significantly reduces administrative burden while improving accuracy.

For example, automated workflows can provision new employees with access to standard applications such as email, HR portals, and collaboration tools based on their department. More specialized access can be granted through approval-based workflows, ensuring that users receive only the permissions necessary for their roles.

By eliminating manual interventions, organizations can reduce delays in access provisioning, enhance operational efficiency, and allow IT teams to focus on higher-value tasks such as security monitoring and threat response.

Compliance and Audit Benefits

Regulatory requirements such as GDPR, HIPAA, and SOX mandate strict control over user access to sensitive data. Automated provisioning and de-provisioning help organizations meet these compliance requirements by enforcing consistent access policies and generating audit trails.

With automation, organizations can:

- Ensure that users are granted only the necessary permissions, reducing the risk of unauthorized access.
- Maintain detailed logs of access changes, providing auditors with transparent records of provisioning and de-provisioning activities.
- Conduct access reviews more efficiently by leveraging automated certification campaigns.

By demonstrating adherence to regulatory requirements, organizations can reduce the risk of non-compliance penalties while strengthening security and governance.

Leveraging AI and Machine Learning in Identity Automation

Artificial intelligence (AI) and machine learning (ML) are transforming the way organizations manage user provisioning and de-provisioning. AI-driven identity analytics can detect anomalies in access patterns, identify excessive privileges, and suggest policy-based adjustments to improve security.

Machine learning models can analyze historical access requests and recommend appropriate access levels for new employees based on similar user profiles. This intelligent automation reduces the need for manual role assignment and enhances the accuracy of provisioning decisions.

Additionally, AI-powered behavioral analytics can flag suspicious activities, such as an inactive user suddenly requesting access to critical systems. Automated de-provisioning can then be triggered based on predefined risk thresholds, further strengthening security.

Challenges in Automating User Provisioning and De-provisioning

Despite its advantages, implementing automated provisioning and de-provisioning comes with challenges. Organizations must ensure that automation policies are well-defined to prevent over-provisioning or under-provisioning of access. Poorly configured automation rules can lead to employees receiving excessive permissions or being locked out of essential systems.

Another challenge is integrating automation with legacy applications that do not support modern identity management protocols. Some older systems may require custom connectors or manual intervention, limiting the effectiveness of automation.

To overcome these challenges, organizations should:

- Conduct a thorough access policy review before implementing automation.
- Test automation workflows in controlled environments before full deployment.
- Regularly update identity policies to reflect changes in business processes and security requirements.

Future Trends in Identity Automation

The future of user provisioning and de-provisioning is evolving with advancements in identity security. Zero Trust security models emphasize continuous verification of user identities, making automated identity governance even more critical. Organizations are adopting Just-In-Time (JIT) provisioning, where access is granted only when needed and revoked automatically after a predefined period.

As organizations move toward passwordless authentication, identity automation will play a central role in managing credential lifecycles, reducing reliance on traditional password-based authentication methods.

By embracing automated provisioning and de-provisioning, organizations can strengthen security, improve efficiency, and ensure compliance with regulatory standards. As technology evolves, identity automation will become even more sophisticated, driving the next generation of secure and efficient access management solutions.

Centralizing Access Certification and Attestation

Access certification and attestation are essential components of Identity Governance and Administration (IGA), ensuring that users maintain appropriate access to systems, applications, and data. Without a structured approach to verifying access rights, organizations face increased security risks, regulatory non-compliance, and operational inefficiencies. Centralizing these processes provides greater control, visibility, and consistency, enabling organizations to enforce security policies effectively while reducing administrative burdens.

Traditional access certification methods often involve manual processes that are time-consuming and prone to errors. Managers are typically required to review and approve user access for multiple systems, leading to inconsistent enforcement and compliance gaps. Decentralized attestation processes can result in oversight failures, as different departments may interpret policies differently or fail to conduct regular reviews. By centralizing access certification and attestation, organizations establish a standardized, auditable framework that enhances both security and accountability.

A centralized approach ensures that all user access reviews follow predefined policies and workflows. Organizations can define criteria for periodic certification campaigns, specifying which access rights must be reviewed, how frequently reviews should occur, and who is responsible for approvals. These campaigns can be automated to trigger at regular intervals, reducing reliance on manual tracking and follow-ups. Automated reminders and escalations help ensure timely completion, minimizing delays and compliance risks.

Regulatory requirements play a significant role in driving the need for centralized access certification. Regulations such as the General Data Protection Regulation (GDPR), the Sarbanes-Oxley Act (SOX), the Health Insurance Portability and Accountability Act (HIPAA), and the Payment Card Industry Data Security Standard (PCI DSS) mandate strict access controls and periodic reviews of user privileges. A fragmented approach to access attestation makes it difficult to demonstrate compliance, as organizations struggle to provide consistent audit logs and verification records. Centralizing access certification enables organizations to maintain comprehensive reports, demonstrating compliance during audits and reducing the risk of penalties.

Beyond compliance, centralization enhances security by reducing the likelihood of unauthorized access. Employees often accumulate access rights over time, particularly when they change roles or work on multiple projects. Without regular reviews, excessive permissions can go unnoticed, increasing the risk of insider threats or external breaches. A centralized system ensures that managers and security teams can easily identify and revoke unnecessary access, enforcing the principle of least privilege across the organization.

Automation plays a critical role in centralizing access certification and attestation. Modern IGA solutions integrate with enterprise applications, directories, and cloud services to aggregate access data into a single platform. These solutions provide dashboards and analytics that offer real-time insights into access patterns, helping organizations detect anomalies and enforce policies more effectively. Instead of manually reviewing spreadsheets or fragmented records, decision-makers can access a consolidated view of user entitlements, making the certification process more efficient and accurate.

Risk-based access reviews further improve the effectiveness of centralized certification programs. Rather than treating all access reviews equally, organizations can prioritize high-risk permissions and critical systems. Advanced analytics and artificial intelligence (AI) capabilities allow organizations to assess the likelihood of misuse or security incidents based on user behavior, role changes, and historical patterns. This targeted approach ensures that resources are focused on mitigating the most significant risks, rather than conducting unnecessary or redundant reviews.

Another benefit of centralizing access certification is improved accountability. A well-defined attestation process ensures that managers and system owners take responsibility for approving or revoking access. With clear audit trails, organizations can track who approved specific permissions, when certifications were conducted, and whether any exceptions were made. This level of transparency not only strengthens security but also simplifies forensic investigations in the event of a security breach.

User experience is another important consideration when implementing a centralized access certification system.

Overburdening managers with excessive certification requests can lead to "rubber-stamping," where approvals are granted without thorough review. To avoid this, organizations should implement streamlined workflows that present access information in an intuitive and digestible format. Providing context, such as the business justification for access and recent usage patterns, allows reviewers to make informed decisions without unnecessary complexity.

Integration with existing identity governance frameworks ensures that centralizing access certification does not create operational silos. Organizations must align attestation workflows with their broader identity management processes, including role-based access control (RBAC), policy-based access control (PBAC), and privileged access management (PAM). By incorporating access certification into the overall identity governance strategy, organizations create a cohesive approach to managing user identities, reducing security gaps, and improving overall efficiency.

While centralizing access certification provides numerous benefits, organizations must also address challenges such as resistance to change and initial implementation complexity. Employees and managers may be accustomed to decentralized processes and require training on new certification workflows. Change management initiatives, including clear communication and user training, help ease the transition and encourage adoption. Additionally, selecting the right technology solution is crucial for success. Organizations should evaluate IGA platforms based on scalability, integration capabilities, automation features, and reporting functionalities to ensure a smooth implementation.

As digital transformation accelerates and organizations adopt hybrid and multi-cloud environments, access certification and attestation become even more critical. Centralized certification provides a scalable framework that adapts to evolving business needs, enabling enterprises to maintain control over access rights across diverse systems and platforms. By leveraging automation, analytics, and standardized policies, organizations strengthen security, reduce compliance risks, and improve operational efficiency.

Privileged Access Management (PAM) and IGA

Privileged Access Management (PAM) and Identity Governance and Administration (IGA) are two critical components of modern identity security frameworks. As organizations expand their IT infrastructures across on-premises and cloud environments, managing privileged accounts has become more complex and crucial for security. Privileged accounts, such as those assigned to system administrators, IT security personnel, and database managers, provide elevated access to critical systems and sensitive data. Without proper oversight, these accounts can become targets for cyber threats, leading to data breaches, regulatory violations, and operational disruptions. By integrating PAM with IGA, organizations can establish a comprehensive security model that ensures privileged access is properly governed, monitored, and controlled.

Privileged Access Management focuses on securing and managing accounts with elevated permissions. These accounts typically have administrative control over servers, databases, networking devices, and cloud platforms, making them valuable targets for malicious actors. Unlike standard user accounts, privileged accounts can bypass security controls, modify system configurations, and access confidential information. If compromised, they pose significant risks to the organization's cybersecurity posture. PAM solutions mitigate these risks by enforcing strict controls, including session monitoring, password vaulting, just-in-time access provisioning, and automated credential rotation.

Identity Governance and Administration provides a broader governance structure for managing digital identities across the enterprise. While PAM specifically addresses privileged users, IGA ensures that all users, including privileged and non-privileged accounts, are assigned appropriate access based on business policies and regulatory requirements. IGA automates identity lifecycle management, access reviews, role assignments, and compliance reporting. By integrating PAM within the IGA framework, organizations can create a unified approach to managing identities and enforcing security policies across all account types.

One of the most critical aspects of PAM and IGA integration is the enforcement of the least privilege principle. This principle ensures that users, including those with administrative roles, only receive the minimum permissions necessary to perform their tasks. Instead of granting persistent access to privileged accounts, PAM enables just-in-time access, where users are granted temporary privileges only when needed. This approach reduces the attack surface by limiting the availability of privileged credentials, making it harder for attackers to exploit them. IGA complements this by enforcing role-based access control (RBAC) and policy-based access control (PBAC), ensuring that privileged users do not accumulate excessive permissions over time.

Access certification and attestation processes also play a key role in managing privileged access. IGA solutions enable organizations to conduct periodic access reviews, ensuring that privileged accounts are assigned only to authorized users. PAM solutions further enhance this process by providing detailed audit logs and real-time monitoring of privileged session activities. By combining these capabilities, security teams can detect anomalies, revoke unnecessary privileges, and ensure continuous compliance with industry regulations.

Another critical component of PAM and IGA integration is privileged session monitoring. PAM solutions record and analyze privileged user activities to identify potential security threats. These sessions can be reviewed in real-time or archived for forensic analysis in case of an incident. By feeding session data into IGA systems, organizations can correlate access patterns with identity governance policies, helping to identify risky behavior and enforce corrective actions. Automated alerts and workflow triggers can be configured to flag unauthorized actions, requiring additional verification before privileged users can proceed with high-risk activities.

Regulatory compliance is another driving factor behind PAM and IGA convergence. Many industry regulations, including GDPR, HIPAA, SOX, and PCI DSS, mandate strict control over privileged accounts. Organizations must demonstrate that they have implemented adequate security controls to protect sensitive data and prevent unauthorized access. IGA solutions provide compliance reporting capabilities, generating audit trails that document privileged access approvals, reviews, and revocations. PAM further strengthens compliance efforts by enforcing strict authentication measures, such as multi-factor authentication (MFA) and password rotation policies, ensuring that privileged credentials are protected from unauthorized use.

Cloud adoption has introduced new challenges in privileged access management. As organizations migrate workloads to cloud platforms, traditional PAM solutions must adapt to dynamic, multi-cloud environments. Cloud service providers offer built-in identity and access management (IAM) tools, but they often lack the governance and centralized control required for enterprise security. By integrating cloud-based PAM with IGA, organizations can enforce consistent policies across on-premises and cloud environments, ensuring that privileged access is managed securely regardless of location. Cloud-native PAM solutions also enable ephemeral access controls, where privileged accounts exist only for the duration of a task and are automatically revoked once completed.

Privileged account discovery and risk assessment are essential for organizations looking to improve their security posture. PAM solutions continuously scan IT environments to identify unmanaged or orphaned privileged accounts that could pose security risks. These accounts are then onboarded into the PAM system, where access policies can be enforced. IGA enhances this process by classifying privileged accounts based on risk levels, allowing organizations to prioritize remediation efforts. Risk-based scoring mechanisms help security teams focus on high-risk accounts, applying stricter access controls where necessary.

Automation plays a crucial role in strengthening PAM and IGA processes. Manual management of privileged accounts and governance policies is time-consuming and prone to human error. By automating workflows, organizations can reduce administrative overhead while ensuring that access requests, approvals, and revocations follow predefined security policies. For instance, PAM solutions can automatically grant temporary privileged access based on IGA approval workflows, eliminating the need for manual intervention. Similarly,

IGA can trigger automated de-provisioning of privileged accounts when employees leave the organization, ensuring that former employees do not retain unauthorized access.

As cybersecurity threats continue to evolve, organizations must adopt a proactive approach to privileged access management and identity governance. The convergence of PAM and IGA provides a robust security framework that enhances visibility, enforces compliance, and mitigates risks associated with privileged accounts. By integrating these solutions, businesses can establish a zero-trust security model, where access to critical systems is continuously verified and strictly controlled. As organizations continue to embrace digital transformation, PAM and IGA will remain essential components of a comprehensive identity security strategy.

Managing External and Third-Party Identities

Organizations today rely on a vast ecosystem of external users, including contractors, business partners, suppliers, vendors, and temporary workers. These external identities require access to enterprise systems, data, and applications to perform their roles effectively. Unlike full-time employees, however, external users operate under different security, compliance, and governance requirements. Managing their access while maintaining security, operational efficiency, and regulatory compliance presents a unique challenge. Without proper identity governance, organizations risk unauthorized access, data breaches, and non-compliance with industry regulations.

The complexity of managing third-party identities stems from their temporary or dynamic nature. Unlike employees who follow a structured onboarding and offboarding process, external users often join organizations through different channels, with varying levels of trust and oversight. A contractor may require access for only a few weeks, while a supplier may need long-term access with periodic changes. Without a formalized approach to identity governance, organizations struggle to ensure that access remains appropriate and is revoked when no longer needed. Orphaned accounts—active credentials that remain after a third party's contract ends—pose a significant security risk if left unmanaged.

To mitigate these risks, organizations must establish well-defined policies for onboarding, managing, and de-provisioning external identities. A structured onboarding process ensures that third-party users receive access based on business needs, following the principle of least privilege. Automating this process through identity governance and administration (IGA) solutions reduces administrative burdens and prevents over-provisioning of access rights. Third-party identity onboarding should involve vetting, approval workflows, and predefined access policies that align with security and compliance requirements.

One of the critical aspects of managing external identities is enforcing strict authentication and access controls. Multi-factor authentication (MFA) should be mandatory for all third-party users to reduce the risk of credential compromise. Context-aware access controls, such as geolocation restrictions and device trust levels, further enhance security by ensuring that third-party access aligns with organizational policies. Organizations must also differentiate access rights between internal and external users, preventing external identities from gaining excessive privileges or accessing sensitive systems.

Monitoring and auditing third-party access is essential for maintaining security. Organizations must continuously track and review external user activities to detect anomalies, unauthorized access attempts, or potential security threats. Regular access certifications ensure that third-party identities retain only the permissions necessary for their roles. Automated access reviews help managers validate whether third-party users still require access, reducing the likelihood of lingering permissions.

Integration between IGA solutions and third-party identity providers enhances security and streamlines access management. Many external users authenticate through their own corporate identity systems, requiring federated access management solutions such as Single Sign-On (SSO) and Security Assertion Markup Language (SAML). By integrating third-party identity providers with an enterprise's IGA framework, organizations can enforce consistent access policies without storing unnecessary credentials.

Contract management and legal agreements play a crucial role in defining third-party identity governance. Organizations should formalize agreements that outline security responsibilities, access restrictions, and compliance requirements. These agreements ensure that external partners understand and adhere to security policies, reducing the risk of data exposure or non-compliance with industry regulations. Organizations should also define exit procedures for third-party users, ensuring that de-provisioning occurs immediately when contracts end or partnerships dissolve.

As cloud adoption increases, managing third-party identities becomes even more complex. Many external users require access to cloud-based applications, Software-as-a-Service (SaaS) platforms, and hybrid environments. A centralized identity governance model ensures that third-party access is managed consistently across all platforms, reducing security fragmentation. Cloud-based identity solutions enable organizations to extend identity governance beyond traditional network perimeters, securing access across multi-cloud environments.

Privileged access management (PAM) is another critical component of third-party identity governance. Some external users, such as IT vendors or consultants, may require administrative access to sensitive systems. Granting excessive privileges without proper oversight increases the risk of security breaches. Implementing just-in-time (JIT) access and time-bound privileges ensures that third-party users receive temporary access only when needed. Session recording and monitoring further enhance security by tracking privileged activities and detecting suspicious behavior.

Security incidents involving third-party identities highlight the importance of a robust identity governance framework. Many high-profile breaches have occurred due to compromised vendor credentials or mismanaged third-party access. Organizations must regularly assess their third-party risk exposure and implement proactive security measures to mitigate threats. Conducting security assessments, penetration tests, and compliance audits helps ensure that third-party access remains aligned with evolving security requirements.

Effective management of external and third-party identities requires a balance between security and operational efficiency. Organizations must provide seamless yet secure access while ensuring that governance policies remain enforceable. By leveraging automation, access reviews, and policy enforcement mechanisms, enterprises can reduce security risks and maintain compliance with industry regulations. A comprehensive identity governance strategy ensures that third-party identities are managed with the same level of security and oversight as internal users, protecting critical systems and sensitive data from unauthorized access.

Integrating IGA with Cloud Applications

As organizations increasingly migrate to cloud-based environments, managing identities across multiple platforms has become more complex. Identity Governance and Administration (IGA) plays a critical role in ensuring secure, efficient, and compliant access to cloud applications. Unlike traditional on-premises identity management solutions, cloud applications introduce new challenges, such as decentralized access controls, multi-tenancy, and dynamic provisioning needs. To maintain security and compliance while supporting business agility, enterprises must integrate IGA with their cloud ecosystems effectively.

Cloud applications operate in diverse environments, including Software-as-a-Service (SaaS), Platform-as-a-Service (PaaS), and Infrastructure-as-a-Service (IaaS) models. Each of these service types requires different identity management strategies. SaaS applications, such as Microsoft 365, Salesforce, and ServiceNow, require user provisioning and de-provisioning processes that align with business policies. PaaS and IaaS environments, like Amazon Web Services (AWS) and Microsoft Azure, involve privileged access controls, role-based assignments, and security policies to protect critical infrastructure. Integrating IGA ensures that all these services operate under a unified identity governance framework.

One of the primary challenges in integrating IGA with cloud applications is managing disparate identity repositories. Unlike traditional environments where a centralized directory, such as Active Directory, governs access, cloud services often maintain their own identity stores. This fragmentation increases the risk of inconsistent access controls, orphaned accounts, and security vulnerabilities. A well-implemented IGA solution consolidates these identity stores, enforcing uniform policies and centralizing user identity management across all applications.

Automating user provisioning and de-provisioning is a key advantage of integrating IGA with cloud applications. When employees join an organization, they require immediate access to collaboration tools, productivity applications, and business systems. Delays in granting access can impact productivity, while manual processes introduce the risk of errors. IGA automates these tasks by linking cloud applications to HR systems and identity providers, ensuring that users receive appropriate permissions based on their roles. Similarly, when employees leave or change roles, IGA enforces immediate de-provisioning, reducing the risk of lingering access rights that could be exploited.

Role-based access control (RBAC) and policy-based access control (PBAC) become even more critical in cloud environments. Cloud applications often support different permission models, which can complicate access governance. RBAC assigns permissions based on predefined roles, ensuring that users receive only the necessary access to perform their jobs. PBAC extends this by incorporating contextual factors such as device type, location, and authentication strength. By integrating IGA with cloud applications, organizations can enforce consistent access policies across all platforms, preventing privilege creep and reducing security risks.

Multi-factor authentication (MFA) and adaptive authentication are also key components of IGA integration with cloud services. Cloud applications are frequently accessed from various locations and devices, making traditional authentication methods insufficient. MFA enhances security by requiring additional verification steps, such as biometrics or one-time passwords. Adaptive authentication further improves security by analyzing user behavior and adjusting authentication requirements based on risk levels. IGA solutions that integrate with cloud applications leverage these mechanisms to ensure secure access while maintaining a seamless user experience.

Compliance and regulatory requirements drive the need for comprehensive identity governance in cloud environments. Regulations such as GDPR, HIPAA, and SOX mandate strict access controls and audit trails to protect sensitive data. Cloud applications, however, introduce compliance challenges due to their distributed nature. Integrating IGA provides organizations with visibility into who has access to what data, when they accessed it, and how permissions were granted. This level of oversight enables businesses to demonstrate compliance and respond to audit requests efficiently.

Privileged access management (PAM) is another critical aspect of IGA integration with cloud applications. Cloud platforms often grant elevated privileges to administrators, developers, and IT staff, creating potential security vulnerabilities if not managed properly. Integrating IGA with PAM solutions ensures that privileged accounts are closely monitored, with access granted only when necessary and revoked immediately after use. This just-in-time (JIT) approach to privilege management minimizes the risk of credential abuse and insider threats.

API-based integrations play a significant role in connecting IGA solutions with cloud applications. Modern cloud services expose identity and access management functions through APIs, allowing seamless communication between IGA platforms and SaaS, PaaS, or IaaS solutions. By leveraging APIs, organizations can automate identity synchronization, enforce security policies, and retrieve access logs in real-time. This integration capability enables greater agility and responsiveness in managing cloud identities.

As organizations expand their cloud adoption, identity federation and single sign-on (SSO) become essential for managing access efficiently. Federation allows users to authenticate once and gain access to multiple cloud applications without re-entering credentials. SSO simplifies authentication while maintaining security, reducing the need for multiple passwords and decreasing the likelihood of credential-based attacks. When integrated with IGA, these capabilities streamline identity management, improving both security and user experience.

Monitoring and analytics further enhance the integration of IGA with cloud applications. Identity analytics leverage machine learning and behavioral analysis to detect anomalies in access patterns. For example, an IGA solution can flag an unusual login attempt from a foreign country or detect excessive privilege escalations within a cloud environment. By integrating analytics into identity governance, organizations can proactively mitigate security threats and enforce risk-based access controls.

Hybrid IT environments add complexity to IGA and cloud integration. Many organizations operate a mix of on-premises and cloud applications, requiring a hybrid approach to identity governance. IGA solutions that support hybrid deployments enable seamless management of both on-premises and cloud identities. This ensures that access policies remain consistent across all environments, reducing security gaps and simplifying identity administration.

A successful integration of IGA with cloud applications requires a strategic approach. Organizations must assess their existing identity infrastructure, define clear governance policies, and select IGA solutions that offer flexible cloud support. Investing in automation, analytics, and API-driven integrations enhances efficiency, security, and compliance. As cloud adoption continues to grow, identity governance will remain a cornerstone of enterprise security, ensuring that access is controlled, monitored, and optimized for the evolving digital landscape.

Handling Hybrid and Multi-Cloud Environments

As organizations adopt digital transformation strategies, the use of hybrid and multi-cloud environments has become increasingly prevalent. Businesses no longer rely solely on on-premises infrastructure; instead, they leverage a combination of private clouds, public clouds, and on-premises systems to optimize performance, scalability, and cost-efficiency. While this shift provides significant benefits, it also introduces complex challenges in security, identity management, and regulatory compliance. Ensuring consistent identity governance and access control across multiple environments requires a strategic approach that aligns with enterprise security policies and business objectives.

Hybrid environments combine on-premises data centers with cloud services, allowing organizations to extend their existing infrastructure while benefiting from the agility of cloud computing. Multi-cloud environments, on the other hand, involve using multiple cloud providers such as AWS, Microsoft Azure, and Google Cloud to avoid vendor lock-in, increase redundancy, and optimize workloads. Managing identities across these diverse platforms requires a unified governance framework that ensures users have appropriate access while maintaining security controls. Without proper governance, businesses risk identity sprawl, unauthorized access, and compliance violations.

Identity Governance and Administration (IGA) solutions play a crucial role in securing hybrid and multi-cloud environments by centralizing identity management. A well-implemented IGA framework provides visibility into all user identities, enabling organizations to enforce consistent access policies regardless of where applications and data reside. By integrating IGA with cloud identity providers, businesses can streamline identity lifecycle management, automate provisioning and de-provisioning, and ensure that access rights are assigned based on business policies rather than individual cloud platform configurations.

One of the major challenges in managing hybrid and multi-cloud identities is the inconsistency of access control mechanisms across different platforms. Cloud providers implement their own identity and access management (IAM) solutions, making it difficult to enforce uniform security policies. AWS Identity and Access Management (IAM), Azure Active Directory (Azure AD), and Google Cloud Identity provide powerful native controls, but they often operate in silos, requiring additional tools to ensure cross-platform security. Centralized identity governance bridges this gap by integrating with these IAM solutions, allowing organizations to enforce consistent role-based access control (RBAC) and policy-based access control (PBAC) across all cloud and on-premises resources.

Security risks increase when organizations fail to properly manage privileged accounts in hybrid and multi-cloud environments. IT administrators, developers, and third-party vendors often require elevated access to configure cloud services, manage workloads, and troubleshoot issues. Without proper controls, privileged credentials can become a target for cybercriminals or be misused internally. Privileged Access Management (PAM) solutions integrated with IGA frameworks help mitigate these risks by enforcing just-in-time access, session monitoring, and automated credential rotation. By limiting the time and scope of privileged access, organizations reduce the attack surface while maintaining operational flexibility.

Regulatory compliance adds another layer of complexity to hybrid and multi-cloud identity management. Regulations such as GDPR, HIPAA, and SOX require strict controls over user access and data protection, regardless of whether data is stored on-premises or in the cloud. Organizations must ensure that access certification, audit logging, and security controls remain consistent across all platforms. IGA solutions provide automated compliance reporting, helping businesses demonstrate adherence to regulatory standards while minimizing manual oversight.

As enterprises scale their hybrid and multi-cloud deployments, identity lifecycle management becomes increasingly important. Employees, contractors, and partners require access to cloud applications and on-premises resources, often with different levels of access based on their roles. Without automation, provisioning and de-provisioning become cumbersome and error-prone, leading to over-provisioned accounts and security vulnerabilities. Automating identity lifecycle management through IGA platforms ensures that users receive appropriate access upon onboarding and have their privileges revoked promptly when they leave or change roles.

Cloud security best practices emphasize the principle of least privilege, ensuring that users and applications have only the permissions necessary to perform their tasks. Applying least privilege principles across hybrid and multi-cloud environments requires continuous monitoring and real-time adjustments to access rights. AI-driven identity analytics enhance security by detecting unusual access patterns, identifying excessive permissions, and recommending corrective actions. By leveraging AI for identity governance, organizations can proactively address security risks and maintain compliance without relying solely on manual access reviews.

Zero Trust security models have gained traction as a means of securing hybrid and multi-cloud environments. Unlike traditional perimeter-based security approaches, Zero Trust assumes that threats exist both inside and outside the network, requiring continuous verification of user identities and device security. Implementing Zero Trust in a hybrid or multi-cloud architecture involves enforcing multi-factor authentication (MFA), micro-segmentation, and risk-based access control. IGA platforms support Zero Trust by providing centralized policy enforcement, ensuring that users must authenticate and validate their permissions before accessing sensitive resources.

Collaboration between IT, security, and compliance teams is essential for successfully managing hybrid and multi-cloud identities. IT teams must align identity governance strategies with cloud architecture decisions, while security teams must continuously monitor for risks and enforce access policies. Compliance teams play a vital role in ensuring that identity governance frameworks meet regulatory requirements and industry standards. A coordinated approach ensures that hybrid and multi-cloud environments remain secure, compliant, and efficient.

Organizations adopting hybrid and multi-cloud architectures must embrace a forward-thinking identity governance strategy that integrates automation, AI-driven security, and Zero Trust principles. As cloud adoption continues to grow, businesses that invest in a centralized and scalable identity governance framework will be better positioned to manage risks, streamline access control, and maintain regulatory compliance across their evolving IT landscapes.

Achieving Compliance through IGA

Regulatory compliance is a key driver for organizations implementing Identity Governance and Administration (IGA). Businesses across industries must comply with various regulations that mandate strict controls over user access, data protection, and security policies. Achieving compliance is not only about meeting regulatory requirements but also about ensuring operational integrity, protecting sensitive data, and maintaining customer trust. Without a structured identity governance framework, organizations risk security breaches, financial penalties, and reputational damage.

IGA helps organizations enforce compliance by automating identity and access management processes, ensuring that access to systems and data is governed by policies aligned with regulatory standards. Many regulations, including the General Data Protection Regulation (GDPR), the Sarbanes-Oxley Act (SOX), the Health Insurance Portability and Accountability Act (HIPAA), and the Payment Card Industry Data Security Standard (PCI DSS), impose stringent requirements on how identities are managed, how access is granted, and how security risks are mitigated. A well-implemented IGA framework provides the necessary oversight to enforce compliance, monitor access, and generate audit-ready reports.

One of the most critical aspects of compliance is ensuring that access is granted based on business needs and regularly reviewed for appropriateness. Excessive permissions or unchecked access to sensitive data can lead to compliance violations and security incidents. IGA solutions enable organizations to enforce role-based access control (RBAC) and policy-based access control (PBAC), ensuring that users receive only the permissions required for their job functions. By defining roles and automating access provisioning, IGA reduces the risk of privilege creep and unauthorized access.

Access certification and attestation are essential for maintaining compliance. Regulations often require organizations to conduct periodic access reviews to confirm that users still require the permissions they have been granted. Without a structured approach, these reviews can be time-consuming and error-prone. IGA automates access certifications by initiating periodic review campaigns, allowing managers and compliance officers to verify user access efficiently. This process ensures that orphaned accounts and excessive permissions are identified and remediated before they become security risks.

Auditability is another key compliance requirement that IGA addresses. Organizations must maintain detailed records of user access, authentication attempts, and privilege escalations to demonstrate adherence to regulatory requirements. IGA solutions provide centralized logging and reporting capabilities, ensuring that all identity-related activities are documented and easily accessible for audits. Real-time monitoring and analytics further enhance compliance efforts by identifying anomalies, detecting unauthorized access attempts, and triggering alerts for suspicious behavior.

Separation of duties (SoD) policies play a critical role in achieving compliance, particularly in financial, healthcare, and government sectors. SoD ensures that no single individual has excessive control over critical business processes, reducing the risk of fraud and errors. IGA enforces SoD by defining conflicting access rights and preventing users from acquiring permissions that violate compliance policies. Automated SoD checks ensure that access requests undergo proper validation before being approved, minimizing compliance risks.

Privileged access management (PAM) integration is another crucial component of IGA compliance strategies. Regulations often require organizations to implement strict controls over privileged accounts, which have elevated access to critical systems and sensitive data. PAM solutions work alongside IGA to ensure that privileged access is granted only when necessary, monitored in real time, and revoked after the task is completed. By integrating PAM with IGA, organizations strengthen compliance by enforcing least privilege principles and reducing the risk of privilege abuse.

Data privacy regulations such as GDPR and the California Consumer Privacy Act (CCPA) impose strict guidelines on how organizations collect, process, and store personal data. IGA ensures compliance with these regulations by enforcing access policies that restrict unauthorized access to sensitive information. Identity analytics and access monitoring help organizations detect and mitigate potential data privacy violations before they escalate into compliance breaches.

The increasing adoption of cloud applications and remote work environments has introduced new compliance challenges. Organizations must ensure that identity governance extends beyond traditional on-premises systems to cloud platforms, SaaS applications, and hybrid environments. IGA solutions integrate with cloud identity providers to enforce consistent access policies across all platforms, ensuring that cloud-based resources are governed with the same level of security and compliance as on-premises systems.

Regulatory frameworks continue to evolve, requiring organizations to adopt a proactive approach to compliance. A static approach to identity governance is insufficient, as new threats and regulatory changes demand continuous adaptation. Organizations must leverage automation, artificial intelligence, and machine learning to enhance their compliance efforts. AI-driven identity analytics can detect unusual access patterns, recommend access adjustments, and automate risk assessments, ensuring that organizations remain compliant with evolving security and regulatory requirements.

Compliance is not solely an IT responsibility but requires collaboration across business units, legal teams, and risk management departments. IGA facilitates this collaboration by providing centralized visibility into identity and access management processes, allowing organizations to align security policies with regulatory requirements. By fostering a compliance-first culture, businesses can reduce risk exposure, improve operational efficiency, and maintain trust with customers, partners, and regulatory bodies.

The cost of non-compliance can be severe, with financial penalties, legal consequences, and reputational damage affecting organizations that fail to implement proper identity governance. IGA provides the necessary tools to enforce access controls, conduct regular audits, and ensure that compliance requirements are met with minimal disruption to business operations. Organizations that prioritize identity governance as part of their compliance strategy are better equipped to navigate regulatory challenges, mitigate security risks, and build a resilient security posture.

Auditing and Reporting in IGA

Auditing and reporting are fundamental components of Identity Governance and Administration (IGA), ensuring that organizations maintain control over user access, comply with regulatory requirements, and detect security risks in real-time. As enterprises grow and their IT environments become increasingly complex, the ability to track, analyze, and report on identity-related activities becomes critical. A well-implemented auditing and reporting framework not only enhances security but also provides transparency and accountability in identity management.

Organizations operate in a landscape where cyber threats, insider risks, and compliance violations pose significant challenges. Without a structured approach to auditing, businesses may struggle to detect unauthorized access, privilege escalations, or policy violations before they result in security breaches. Auditing in IGA enables organizations to monitor who has access to what systems, when access was granted, how it is being used, and whether it aligns with established policies. By continuously tracking access patterns and changes, security teams can identify anomalies, revoke excessive permissions, and enforce compliance.

Regulatory compliance is one of the primary drivers for robust auditing and reporting within IGA. Organizations in industries such as healthcare, finance, and government must comply with regulations like GDPR, HIPAA, SOX, and PCI DSS, which mandate strict access control measures and detailed audit logs. Failure to meet these compliance requirements can result in legal penalties, financial losses, and reputational damage. IGA solutions help businesses generate audit-ready reports that demonstrate adherence to security policies, ensuring that access management processes are well-documented and verifiable.

A key aspect of auditing in IGA is access certification, which involves periodic reviews of user entitlements. Managers and system owners must verify that employees, contractors, and third-party users have the appropriate level of access based on their job roles and responsibilities. Regular access reviews reduce the risk of privilege creep, where users accumulate excessive permissions over time. Automated certification campaigns streamline this process by notifying reviewers, collecting approvals or revocations, and generating audit logs that document compliance actions.

Privileged access management (PAM) is another critical area where auditing plays a vital role. Privileged accounts, such as those belonging to system administrators and IT security personnel, have elevated access to critical systems and data. If these accounts are not properly governed, they can become a major security risk. IGA solutions integrate with PAM tools to monitor privileged sessions, track command execution, and generate reports detailing every action taken by privileged users. This level of oversight ensures that administrative access is justified, monitored, and audited for security and compliance purposes.

Real-time monitoring and anomaly detection enhance the effectiveness of IGA auditing by identifying suspicious activities as they occur. Traditional auditing methods often rely on scheduled reviews, which may not be sufficient for detecting threats in fast-moving environments. Advanced IGA platforms incorporate artificial intelligence and machine learning to analyze behavioral patterns, detect unusual access requests, and flag potential security risks. For example, if a user suddenly accesses a sensitive database outside of normal working hours from an unfamiliar location, the system can trigger an alert and prompt an immediate security review.

Comprehensive reporting capabilities are essential for translating audit data into actionable insights. IGA solutions provide dashboards and customizable reports that allow security teams, compliance officers, and executives to visualize identity-related activities. These reports can include metrics such as failed login attempts, excessive permission assignments, access request trends, and policy violations. Having a centralized reporting system ensures that organizations can quickly generate compliance reports, track security incidents, and make informed decisions to improve identity governance.

Audit logs must also be retained for extended periods to support forensic investigations and compliance audits. Many regulatory frameworks require businesses to store identity-related logs for months or even years. Secure log storage, coupled with tamper-proof mechanisms, ensures that historical access data remains available for auditing purposes. Organizations should implement best practices for log management, including encryption, access controls, and redundancy to prevent data loss or manipulation.

Integration with Security Information and Event Management (SIEM) systems further strengthens auditing and reporting in IGA. SIEM solutions collect and analyze security events from across the enterprise, correlating identity-related data with other security incidents. By integrating IGA audit logs with SIEM platforms, organizations gain a holistic view of security risks, enabling them to detect insider threats, prevent fraud, and respond to incidents more effectively.

User awareness and training also play an important role in ensuring that auditing and reporting processes remain effective. Employees, managers, and IT administrators must understand the importance of accurate access records and compliance with certification campaigns. Organizations should establish clear policies regarding audit participation, security best practices, and reporting of suspicious activities. A culture of accountability reinforces identity governance efforts and reduces the likelihood of security oversights.

As cloud adoption continues to grow, auditing and reporting in IGA must adapt to hybrid and multi-cloud environments. Organizations leveraging SaaS, PaaS, and IaaS solutions must ensure that identity governance extends beyond traditional on-premises systems. Cloud-native IGA solutions provide real-time visibility into access activities across multiple platforms, helping organizations enforce consistent security policies regardless of where applications and data reside.

Auditing and reporting are not just about compliance; they are essential for maintaining a strong security posture. By continuously monitoring access, enforcing governance policies, and leveraging data-driven insights, organizations can reduce security risks, enhance operational efficiency, and demonstrate regulatory adherence. A proactive approach to auditing within IGA ensures that identity governance remains a dynamic and integral part of an organization's cybersecurity strategy.

Auditing and Reporting in IGA

Auditing and reporting are essential components of Identity Governance and Administration (IGA), providing organizations with the ability to track, monitor, and analyze identity-related activities across their IT environments. As businesses grow and adopt cloud, hybrid, and multi-cloud architectures, maintaining control over user access and security policies becomes increasingly complex. A robust auditing and reporting framework ensures that organizations can enforce compliance, detect security risks, and respond effectively to identity-related threats.

One of the primary purposes of auditing in IGA is to maintain visibility over user access to enterprise resources. Organizations must be able to track who has access to which systems, when access was granted, and whether access remains appropriate over time. Without a centralized auditing mechanism, businesses risk security breaches due to privilege creep, orphaned accounts, or unauthorized access. By continuously logging identity-related activities, organizations can proactively manage security threats, reducing the likelihood of data leaks and insider attacks.

Regulatory compliance requirements drive the need for detailed audit logs and reporting capabilities. Various laws and industry standards, such as the General Data Protection Regulation (GDPR), the Sarbanes-Oxley Act (SOX), the Health Insurance Portability and Accountability

Act (HIPAA), and the Payment Card Industry Data Security Standard (PCI DSS), mandate strict access controls and documentation of identity-related actions. Organizations must demonstrate that access management processes adhere to these regulations by providing audit logs that record authentication attempts, access requests, approvals, privilege escalations, and account modifications.

Access certification is a key function within IGA that supports auditing efforts. Organizations must conduct periodic reviews to verify that users retain only the access necessary for their job functions. Managers and security teams are responsible for attesting to the validity of assigned permissions, ensuring that no excessive or unnecessary access persists. Automated access certification campaigns help organizations enforce governance policies while maintaining an auditable record of approval decisions. These reviews play a crucial role in identifying and correcting security risks before they result in compliance violations or security incidents.

Privileged access management (PAM) integration with IGA strengthens auditing efforts by tracking high-risk activities performed by users with elevated permissions. Privileged accounts, such as those belonging to system administrators and IT security teams, pose a significant security risk if not properly governed. By monitoring privileged sessions, recording command executions, and enforcing just-in-time access controls, organizations can reduce the risks associated with privileged accounts. Detailed audit logs ensure that all privileged actions are accounted for, helping organizations identify unauthorized changes or suspicious behavior.

Real-time monitoring and anomaly detection further enhance IGA auditing capabilities by identifying unusual access patterns and potential security threats. Traditional auditing relies on periodic reviews, which may not be sufficient in detecting insider threats or credential-based attacks. Modern IGA solutions leverage artificial intelligence (AI) and machine learning to analyze behavior patterns, flag anomalies, and generate alerts for security teams. If a user attempts to access sensitive data from an unrecognized device or logs in from an unusual geographic location, automated alerts can prompt an immediate investigation.

Effective reporting capabilities transform raw audit data into actionable insights for security teams, compliance officers, and IT administrators. IGA solutions provide dashboards that visualize access trends, compliance status, and security risks. Customizable reports allow organizations to tailor reporting based on regulatory requirements, internal security policies, and audit needs. Reports can include key metrics such as access review completion rates, failed login attempts, excessive permission assignments, and privileged session activities.

Maintaining an audit trail over time is essential for forensic investigations and compliance audits. Many regulations require businesses to retain identity-related logs for extended periods, ensuring that security teams have historical access records when conducting investigations. Secure storage of audit logs, coupled with access controls and encryption, prevents tampering and unauthorized modifications. Implementing log retention policies ensures that compliance obligations are met while keeping storage costs manageable.

Integration with Security Information and Event Management (SIEM) solutions enhances IGA auditing by correlating identity events with other security incidents. SIEM platforms aggregate and analyze security data from various sources, helping organizations detect advanced threats that involve identity-based attacks. By integrating IGA audit logs with SIEM solutions, businesses gain a holistic view of security risks, improving their ability to respond to incidents efficiently.

User awareness and training play a significant role in ensuring that auditing and reporting processes are effective. Employees, managers, and IT administrators must understand the importance of accurate access records and their role in maintaining security compliance. Organizations should establish clear policies regarding audit participation, access review responsibilities, and best practices for reporting suspicious activities. A culture of accountability strengthens identity governance efforts and reduces the likelihood of security oversights.

As enterprises expand their reliance on cloud services, auditing and reporting in IGA must evolve to address new challenges in managing identities across distributed environments. Cloud-native IGA solutions provide real-time visibility into user access across multiple platforms, helping organizations enforce security policies consistently. The adoption of Zero Trust security principles, which emphasize continuous verification and least privilege access, further reinforces the need for real-time auditing and adaptive reporting mechanisms.

A well-defined auditing and reporting strategy in IGA enables organizations to maintain security, ensure compliance, and optimize identity governance processes. By leveraging automation, AI-driven analytics, and centralized access controls, businesses can proactively manage identity risks while improving operational efficiency. A strong focus on auditing and reporting helps organizations create a resilient security framework, capable of adapting to evolving regulatory requirements and emerging cyber threats.

Protecting Sensitive Data with IGA

Sensitive data is one of the most valuable assets for any organization, but it is also one of the most vulnerable. With increasing cyber threats, regulatory requirements, and the complexities of modern IT environments, organizations must take a proactive approach to data security. Identity Governance and Administration (IGA) plays a crucial role in protecting sensitive data by ensuring that access is granted only to authorized users, monitored continuously, and revoked when no longer needed. A strong IGA framework enhances security, reduces risks, and helps organizations meet compliance obligations while maintaining operational efficiency.

Data breaches and insider threats remain a major concern for businesses, governments, and institutions handling confidential information. Unauthorized access to sensitive data can lead to financial losses, reputational damage, and legal consequences. IGA solutions address these risks by enforcing strict access controls, ensuring that users receive only the permissions necessary for their job functions. Role-based access control (RBAC) and policy-based access control (PBAC) mechanisms prevent excessive privileges, reducing the likelihood of data exposure. By implementing least privilege principles, organizations can ensure that users have only the minimum access required to perform their tasks, minimizing potential attack surfaces.

The rapid adoption of cloud services and remote work environments has further complicated data protection efforts. Employees, contractors, and third-party vendors access corporate resources from various locations and devices, increasing the risk of unauthorized data access. IGA solutions help organizations centralize identity management across cloud applications, on-premises systems, and hybrid environments. By integrating with identity providers and enforcing consistent access policies, businesses can maintain a unified security posture, regardless of where data resides. This prevents unauthorized access and ensures that sensitive information is protected across all platforms.

Automated provisioning and de-provisioning are essential for securing sensitive data. When employees join an organization, they require access to systems, databases, and applications containing confidential information. Manual access management processes are inefficient and prone to human error, leading to potential security gaps. IGA automates the onboarding process, ensuring that new users receive appropriate access based on predefined policies. Similarly, when employees leave or change roles, automated de-provisioning ensures that access to sensitive data is revoked immediately, reducing the risk of lingering permissions that could be exploited by malicious actors.

Access certification and periodic reviews play a significant role in protecting sensitive data. Over time, users may accumulate excessive permissions due to role changes, project-based access, or emergency access requests. Without regular oversight, these permissions can go unnoticed, increasing the risk of unauthorized data exposure. IGA enables organizations to conduct automated access reviews, requiring managers and security teams to validate whether users still need access to sensitive systems. By continuously reviewing and adjusting permissions, businesses can prevent privilege creep and ensure compliance with internal security policies and regulatory requirements.

Privileged Access Management (PAM) integration further enhances data protection by securing high-risk accounts. Privileged users, such as system administrators and IT security personnel, often have access to critical systems and sensitive databases. If these accounts are compromised, attackers can gain unrestricted access to confidential data. IGA works alongside PAM solutions to enforce strict controls over privileged accounts, implementing just-in-time access, session monitoring, and automated credential rotation. This ensures that privileged users can only access sensitive data when necessary and that their activities are logged for audit purposes.

Compliance with data protection regulations is another driving factor for implementing IGA. Various laws, including the General Data Protection Regulation (GDPR), the Health Insurance Portability and Accountability Act (HIPAA), and the California Consumer Privacy Act (CCPA), mandate strict access controls and data protection measures. Organizations must demonstrate that they have implemented effective security policies to protect personal and financial information. IGA solutions provide audit trails, access reports, and compliance dashboards that help businesses meet regulatory requirements and respond to audit requests efficiently. By maintaining detailed records of access logs, identity changes, and certification campaigns, organizations can prove their commitment to data security and compliance.

Data loss prevention (DLP) strategies can be strengthened with IGA by enforcing security policies at the identity level. Traditional DLP solutions focus on monitoring and blocking unauthorized data transfers, but without identity governance, they may not provide full visibility into who has access to sensitive files. IGA enhances DLP by ensuring that access rights align with business policies, preventing unauthorized data sharing or accidental exposure. Combining IGA with DLP allows organizations to create a multi-layered defense strategy that protects sensitive data from both external threats and insider risks.

Artificial intelligence and machine learning are transforming IGA by enabling proactive threat detection. Advanced identity analytics analyze access patterns, user behavior, and risk indicators to detect potential security threats before they escalate. If an employee suddenly accesses a large volume of sensitive data outside of normal working hours, AI-powered IGA solutions can flag the activity as suspicious and trigger security actions, such as requiring additional authentication or temporarily revoking access. These intelligent capabilities help organizations strengthen their security posture by responding to risks in real time.

User awareness and training remain critical components of data protection. Even with advanced security technologies in place, human error remains one of the leading causes of data breaches. Employees must understand the importance of secure access management, password hygiene, and recognizing phishing attempts. IGA supports security awareness initiatives by enforcing strong authentication policies, requiring periodic password changes, and providing self-service portals for users to manage their credentials securely. Educating employees about data security best practices ensures that identity governance efforts are reinforced at every level of the organization.

As cyber threats continue to evolve, protecting sensitive data requires a comprehensive and adaptive approach. IGA provides the necessary tools to manage user access, enforce security policies, and maintain compliance in an increasingly complex digital landscape. By implementing a robust IGA framework, organizations can reduce security risks, prevent unauthorized data exposure, and ensure that sensitive information remains protected at all times.

Governance and Risk Management

Governance and risk management play a central role in modern enterprises, ensuring that organizations operate within defined policies, comply with regulatory requirements, and mitigate potential threats. As businesses expand their digital footprints, the complexity of managing risks associated with identity governance, cybersecurity, and compliance increases. A well-structured governance and risk management framework helps organizations maintain operational resilience while addressing evolving security challenges.

Effective governance provides a structured approach to decision-making, aligning business objectives with security policies and regulatory compliance. Organizations must define clear governance models that establish accountability for identity and access management (IAM), cybersecurity, and data protection. These models outline roles and responsibilities for executives, IT administrators, compliance officers, and other stakeholders involved in risk management. Without a strong governance structure, businesses risk inefficiencies, security breaches, and non-compliance with industry regulations.

Risk management involves identifying, assessing, and mitigating risks that could impact an organization's operations, reputation, or financial stability. In the context of identity governance, risks often arise from unauthorized access, privilege mismanagement, insider threats, and non-compliant user behavior. Organizations must conduct regular risk assessments to evaluate potential vulnerabilities in their identity and access management processes. By analyzing access patterns, reviewing user privileges, and implementing automated risk-scoring mechanisms, businesses can proactively address security threats before they escalate.

Regulatory compliance is a key driver of governance and risk management. Governments and industry regulators impose strict requirements on organizations to ensure the protection of sensitive data, financial integrity, and consumer privacy. Regulations such as the General Data Protection Regulation (GDPR), the Sarbanes-Oxley Act (SOX), the Health Insurance Portability and Accountability Act (HIPAA), and the Payment Card Industry Data Security Standard (PCI DSS) mandate strong governance controls. Organizations that fail to comply with these regulations face financial penalties, legal consequences, and reputational damage. Implementing a governance framework that aligns with regulatory standards helps businesses avoid compliance violations while strengthening overall security.

Identity Governance and Administration (IGA) plays a critical role in governance and risk management by providing visibility into user identities, access rights, and policy enforcement. IGA solutions enable organizations to automate access certification, enforce role-based and policy-based access controls, and generate audit reports to demonstrate compliance. By centralizing identity governance, businesses can establish consistent policies that reduce security risks while ensuring that access permissions align with business needs.

Privileged access management (PAM) is another essential component of risk management. Privileged accounts have elevated permissions that allow users to modify critical systems, access sensitive data, and configure security settings. If not properly governed, these accounts become prime targets for cyberattacks and insider threats. PAM solutions enforce stringent controls over privileged users, ensuring that access is granted only when necessary and that privileged sessions are monitored for suspicious activity. Integrating PAM with IGA strengthens risk management by reducing the likelihood of unauthorized privilege escalations.

Continuous monitoring and risk analytics enhance governance by providing real-time insights into identity-related threats. Advanced IGA platforms incorporate artificial intelligence (AI) and machine learning to analyze user behavior, detect anomalies, and flag potential security risks. For example, an AI-driven system can identify a user accessing sensitive data outside of normal working hours or detect an account with excessive privileges that deviates from established role-based access controls. These insights enable security teams to respond proactively, reducing the likelihood of security breaches.

Governance frameworks must also account for third-party risk management. Many organizations rely on external contractors, vendors, and partners who require access to corporate resources. Managing third-party identities presents unique challenges, as these users may not follow the same security policies as internal employees. Implementing identity governance policies for third-party users ensures that access is granted based on business requirements, continuously reviewed, and revoked when no longer needed. Organizations must also enforce multi-factor authentication (MFA) and context-aware access controls to mitigate risks associated with external identities.

Crisis management and incident response are integral to a governance and risk management strategy. Despite strong preventive measures, security incidents may still occur, requiring organizations to have a well-defined response plan. Incident response teams should be prepared to investigate identity-related breaches, revoke compromised credentials, and mitigate the impact of security incidents. A robust governance framework includes clear escalation procedures, communication plans, and post-incident reviews to strengthen security resilience.

Cloud adoption introduces additional governance and risk management complexities. Organizations operating in hybrid and multi-cloud environments must ensure that identity governance extends across all platforms. Cloud service providers offer native identity and access management (IAM) tools, but these solutions often lack the centralized visibility required for enterprise-wide governance. By integrating cloud IAM with IGA, businesses can enforce uniform policies, monitor cloud-based access, and mitigate security risks associated with cloud workloads.

Governance and risk management are ongoing processes that require continuous improvement. Organizations must regularly review security policies, update access controls, and conduct compliance audits to adapt to changing regulatory landscapes and emerging threats. Cybersecurity threats evolve rapidly, making it essential for businesses to remain agile in their risk management strategies. By fostering a culture of security awareness and accountability, organizations can strengthen their governance frameworks and reduce vulnerabilities.

Strong governance and risk management practices enable organizations to balance security with business agility. By implementing structured identity governance, automating risk assessments, and enforcing regulatory compliance, businesses can mitigate threats while maintaining operational efficiency. A proactive approach to governance ensures that organizations remain resilient in the face of evolving security challenges and regulatory requirements.

Identity Reconciliation and Conflict Resolution

As organizations grow and their IT environments become increasingly complex, managing digital identities across multiple systems, applications, and directories presents significant challenges. Identity reconciliation and conflict resolution are critical components of Identity Governance and Administration (IGA), ensuring that identity data remains accurate, consistent, and properly governed. Without a structured approach to reconciliation, organizations risk security vulnerabilities, compliance failures, and operational inefficiencies due to conflicting identity records, duplicate accounts, and misaligned access privileges.

Identity reconciliation refers to the process of aggregating, normalizing, and synchronizing identity data from multiple sources to create a unified and accurate representation of user identities. In large enterprises, identity data is often distributed across various identity stores, including on-premises directories, cloud-based applications, human resource systems, and third-party platforms. Discrepancies arise when these systems store inconsistent or outdated identity attributes, leading to access control failures and potential security risks. Effective reconciliation ensures that identity data remains current and aligned across all systems, reducing the likelihood of unauthorized access or privilege escalation.

The reconciliation process begins with data aggregation, where identity attributes from different sources are collected and analyzed. This process involves extracting user records, permissions, group memberships, and role assignments from disparate systems. Aggregated data is then compared to identify mismatches, such as missing attributes, outdated job roles, or duplicate accounts. Advanced identity reconciliation tools leverage machine learning and artificial intelligence to detect anomalies, automatically flagging inconsistencies that require resolution.

Conflicts in identity data occur when mismatched or contradictory records exist across systems. These conflicts can stem from manual entry errors, outdated information, incomplete synchronization processes, or differing identity management policies across departments. A common example is when an employee's role change is updated in an HR system but not reflected in access control lists, resulting in excessive permissions. Conflicts may also arise when a user has multiple accounts across different platforms with varying privilege levels, leading to potential security gaps. Resolving these conflicts is essential to maintain compliance with least privilege principles and ensure proper access governance.

To address identity conflicts, organizations must establish predefined resolution rules that dictate how discrepancies should be handled. Automated conflict resolution mechanisms apply logic-based rules to correct inconsistencies without manual intervention. For instance, if two systems contain different email addresses for the same user, a reconciliation engine may prioritize the authoritative source, such as the HR system, and update other records accordingly. In cases where automatic resolution is not possible, escalation workflows route conflicts to designated administrators or managers for manual review and approval.

One of the key benefits of identity reconciliation is improved security posture. When identity data is inconsistent, unauthorized users may retain access to critical systems even after they leave an organization or change roles. Reconciling identity records ensures that de-provisioning occurs in a timely manner, reducing the risk of insider threats and account misuse. Organizations can also leverage reconciliation reports to audit identity changes, detect policy violations, and ensure compliance with regulatory requirements such as GDPR, HIPAA, and SOX.

Role-based access control (RBAC) and policy-based access control (PBAC) frameworks further enhance identity reconciliation by enforcing consistent access policies. When identity records are aligned with predefined roles, organizations can apply governance rules to automatically update permissions based on role changes. This eliminates the need for manual intervention, streamlining access management while reducing the risk of privilege creep. Additionally, real-time reconciliation allows organizations to enforce just-in-time access provisioning, granting temporary access only when required and revoking it as soon as the task is completed.

Hybrid and multi-cloud environments introduce additional complexity to identity reconciliation efforts. Cloud-based applications often have their own identity stores and authentication mechanisms, making it difficult to maintain consistency across on-premises and cloud platforms. Federated identity management solutions, combined with IGA frameworks, provide a unified approach to reconciliation by synchronizing cloud and on-premises identity data. API-based integrations enable real-time updates across multiple platforms, ensuring that identity attributes remain synchronized regardless of where applications and data reside.

Privileged access management (PAM) also benefits from identity reconciliation by ensuring that privileged accounts are properly tracked and governed. Privileged users, such as IT administrators and security personnel, often have elevated permissions across multiple systems. Without proper reconciliation, dormant or orphaned privileged accounts can become security liabilities. By continuously reconciling privileged access data, organizations can enforce stricter controls over administrative accounts, reducing the risk of credential misuse and insider threats.

Identity reconciliation plays a crucial role in merger and acquisition (M&A) scenarios, where organizations must consolidate identity records from different IT infrastructures. Without a structured reconciliation process, users may experience disruptions, access inconsistencies, or unauthorized access to sensitive systems. By normalizing identity data across merging entities, organizations can ensure a seamless transition while maintaining security and compliance.

Data quality is another important factor in successful identity reconciliation. Organizations must establish data governance policies that define identity attribute standards, naming conventions, and authoritative sources. Poor data quality, such as inconsistent user IDs, incorrect department assignments, or duplicate records, can lead to failed reconciliation efforts. Implementing data validation rules, periodic data cleansing, and continuous monitoring improves the accuracy and reliability of identity data across the enterprise.

Organizations must also consider user experience when implementing identity reconciliation processes. While security and compliance are top priorities, ensuring that users do not encounter unnecessary access delays or disruptions is equally important. A well-implemented reconciliation framework allows employees to seamlessly transition between roles, access new applications without friction, and receive timely updates to their identity attributes. Self-service identity management portals further enhance user experience by allowing employees to verify their access, request updates, and resolve discrepancies without extensive IT involvement.

As cyber threats evolve and regulatory pressures increase, identity reconciliation and conflict resolution will remain vital components of an organization's security strategy. By implementing automated reconciliation mechanisms, enforcing standardized identity governance policies, and leveraging AI-driven analytics, businesses can maintain a strong security posture while improving operational efficiency. A proactive approach to identity reconciliation not only reduces security risks but also ensures that identity governance processes align with business objectives and compliance requirements.

Incorporating AI and Machine Learning in IGA

The rapid evolution of digital transformation has significantly increased the complexity of identity governance and administration (IGA). As enterprises expand their IT environments across cloud, on-premises, and hybrid infrastructures, managing user identities, access privileges, and security policies has become more challenging. Traditional IGA solutions rely on static rules and manual processes, which can be inefficient, error-prone, and slow in responding to evolving security threats. Artificial intelligence (AI) and machine learning (ML) are transforming IGA by introducing intelligent automation, adaptive decision-making, and proactive risk mitigation. These technologies enhance security, improve operational efficiency, and provide deeper insights into identity-related risks.

AI-driven identity governance enables organizations to move beyond static role-based access control (RBAC) and policy-based access control (PBAC). Instead of relying solely on predefined rules, AI continuously analyzes identity data, behavioral patterns, and access requests to dynamically adjust access privileges. This approach reduces the risks of over-provisioning, privilege creep, and unauthorized access. By leveraging machine learning algorithms, IGA systems can detect anomalies, predict potential security risks, and suggest corrective actions, making identity management more adaptive and efficient.

One of the key applications of AI in IGA is intelligent access analytics. Traditional access reviews and certification processes are often time-consuming and prone to human oversight. AI enhances these processes by identifying unusual access patterns, flagging high-risk accounts, and prioritizing access reviews based on real-time risk assessments. Instead of requiring security teams to manually review every access request, AI streamlines the process by highlighting anomalies and providing automated recommendations. This reduces the workload on administrators while improving security and compliance.

Machine learning models also improve the accuracy of identity lifecycle management. Automated provisioning and de-provisioning of user accounts can benefit from AI-driven insights that determine appropriate access levels based on historical data and peer group analysis. For example, when a new employee joins an organization, AI can analyze similar job roles, past access requests, and usage patterns to recommend the optimal set of permissions. If an employee transitions to a new role, ML algorithms can automatically adjust access privileges to reflect the new responsibilities, ensuring that unnecessary permissions are revoked in a timely manner.

Behavioral analytics is another powerful use case for AI in IGA. Traditional security policies rely on predefined access control rules, which may not always detect insider threats or compromised accounts. AI-powered behavioral analytics continuously monitor user activities, comparing them against baseline behaviors. If a user exhibits unusual behavior—such as accessing sensitive systems at odd hours, downloading large volumes of data, or attempting to access unauthorized applications—the system can generate alerts, trigger step-up authentication, or temporarily suspend access until the activity is verified.

AI-driven risk scoring further enhances identity governance by dynamically assessing the risk associated with each user and access request. Machine learning models analyze multiple risk factors, including user location, device type, authentication history, and access behavior, to assign a risk score. High-risk activities may prompt additional authentication steps, while low-risk users can be granted access seamlessly. This adaptive security approach reduces friction for legitimate users while adding extra layers of protection for high-risk scenarios.

The integration of AI and ML in IGA also improves compliance and audit processes. Regulatory requirements mandate strict controls over user access and data protection, requiring organizations to conduct regular audits and generate compliance reports. AI automates compliance monitoring by continuously tracking identity-related activities and identifying potential policy violations. Instead of relying on periodic manual audits, AI-driven IGA solutions provide real-time compliance insights, reducing the risk of non-compliance and streamlining audit preparation.

Another critical advantage of AI in IGA is its ability to detect and mitigate identity-based threats in real time. Traditional security tools often struggle to keep up with sophisticated cyberattacks that exploit compromised credentials or insider threats. AI-driven threat intelligence enhances identity governance by correlating identity data with threat intelligence feeds, security events, and external risk indicators. If AI detects signs of credential compromise—such as an employee's credentials appearing on the dark web—it can automatically trigger security measures, such as requiring a password reset or enforcing multi-factor authentication (MFA).

Self-service identity management is another area where AI enhances user experience while maintaining security. Traditional access request processes often involve lengthy approval chains, creating delays and inefficiencies. AI-powered chatbots and virtual assistants simplify identity management by enabling employees to request access, reset passwords, or check compliance status through natural language interactions. These AI-driven interfaces reduce IT helpdesk workloads while improving user productivity and security.

The application of machine learning in role mining and role optimization is transforming how organizations define and manage user roles. Instead of manually creating and maintaining role definitions, ML algorithms analyze access patterns and organizational structures to suggest optimized role hierarchies. This eliminates redundant roles, reduces excessive permissions, and simplifies access management. By continuously learning from access behaviors, ML ensures that roles remain aligned with evolving business needs, improving security and operational efficiency.

Despite the numerous benefits of AI in IGA, organizations must address challenges such as data privacy, ethical considerations, and the risk of algorithmic bias. AI models rely on vast amounts of identity data, which must be handled securely to prevent exposure or misuse. Transparency in AI decision-making is also critical to ensuring that identity governance policies remain fair and unbiased. Organizations should implement governance frameworks to monitor AI-driven decisions, validate model accuracy, and mitigate potential risks associated with automated identity management.

The adoption of AI and machine learning in IGA represents a shift toward a more proactive, intelligent, and adaptive approach to identity governance. As cyber threats continue to evolve, AI-driven IGA solutions provide organizations with the agility to detect risks, enforce policies dynamically, and enhance user experience without compromising security. By integrating AI into their identity governance strategies, businesses can improve efficiency, strengthen compliance, and build a resilient security framework that adapts to the complexities of modern IT environments.

Managing APIs and Service Accounts

As organizations increasingly rely on automation, cloud services, and interconnected applications, managing APIs and service accounts has become a critical aspect of identity governance and administration (IGA). APIs serve as the backbone of modern applications, enabling seamless integration between systems, while service accounts facilitate automated processes and system interactions. Without proper governance, these accounts can introduce security vulnerabilities, compliance risks, and operational inefficiencies. A structured approach to managing APIs and service accounts ensures secure access, minimizes threats, and maintains compliance with industry regulations.

APIs enable applications to communicate and share data, often handling sensitive transactions such as authentication, user provisioning, and financial operations. Because APIs expose functionality to external and internal systems, improper management can lead to data breaches, unauthorized access, and service disruptions. Organizations must implement strong authentication mechanisms, such as API keys, OAuth tokens, and certificate-based authentication, to secure API access. Additionally, defining role-based and policy-based access controls for APIs ensures that only authorized applications and users can interact with specific endpoints.

Service accounts are non-human identities used by applications, scripts, and services to perform automated tasks. These accounts often have elevated privileges, allowing them to access databases, modify system configurations, or interact with cloud resources. Without proper governance, service accounts can become security liabilities, particularly if they are over-provisioned, misconfigured, or left unmanaged. Implementing strict lifecycle management for service accounts ensures that they are created with minimal privileges, regularly audited, and de-provisioned when no longer needed.

One of the biggest challenges in managing service accounts is visibility. Many organizations struggle to track where service accounts exist, what permissions they hold, and whether they comply with security policies. Centralizing service account management within an IGA framework provides full visibility, enabling administrators to enforce policies, detect anomalies, and revoke unnecessary access. Automated discovery tools can help identify unmanaged service accounts, ensuring that no orphaned accounts persist within the environment.

Privileged access management (PAM) plays a crucial role in securing service accounts. Because these accounts often have broad access, they become attractive targets for attackers seeking to exploit system vulnerabilities. Implementing just-in-time (JIT) access and rotating credentials for service accounts reduces the risk of unauthorized access. PAM solutions can also enforce session monitoring and logging for high-risk service accounts, ensuring that any suspicious activity is detected and addressed in real time.

API security must be reinforced through continuous monitoring and auditing. Organizations should maintain logs of API requests, track failed authentication attempts, and monitor access patterns for anomalies. Security Information and Event Management (SIEM) solutions can integrate with IGA platforms to correlate API activities with other identity-related events, providing a holistic view of security risks. By analyzing API access trends, organizations can detect unauthorized use, enforce throttling limits, and apply risk-based authentication measures.

Compliance requirements add another layer of complexity to API and service account management. Regulations such as GDPR, HIPAA, and PCI DSS mandate strict access controls and audit trails for systems handling sensitive data. Organizations must document API permissions, enforce least privilege principles for service accounts, and generate reports demonstrating compliance. Regular access reviews help ensure that APIs and service accounts maintain only the necessary permissions required for business operations.

The shift to cloud-native environments and containerized applications introduces additional challenges in managing APIs and service accounts. Cloud platforms provide dynamic and ephemeral workloads that require flexible identity governance strategies. Organizations must implement federated identity solutions that enable consistent access controls across on-premises and cloud applications.

Additionally, managing API security across multi-cloud environments requires standardized policies that align with organizational security frameworks.

Zero Trust principles provide a robust framework for securing APIs and service accounts. Instead of assuming trust based on network location, Zero Trust enforces continuous verification of API calls and service account activities. Implementing multi-factor authentication (MFA) for API access, applying attribute-based access controls, and segmenting API traffic reduce the risk of unauthorized interactions. By applying Zero Trust to identity governance, organizations strengthen their security posture while enabling secure automation.

AI-driven identity analytics enhance API and service account governance by identifying deviations from normal behavior. Machine learning models can detect anomalies such as unusual service account logins, excessive API request rates, or privilege escalations. These insights enable security teams to respond proactively, applying policy adjustments or requiring additional authentication when necessary. Automated remediation workflows further improve security by revoking excessive permissions or rotating compromised credentials in response to detected threats.

As organizations continue to expand their digital ecosystems, managing APIs and service accounts remains a fundamental aspect of identity governance. A well-defined strategy that includes strong authentication, centralized visibility, automated lifecycle management, and continuous monitoring ensures that these accounts remain secure and compliant. By integrating IGA principles with modern security frameworks, businesses can mitigate risks while maintaining operational efficiency in an increasingly interconnected world.

Building a Sustainable Governance Model

A sustainable governance model is essential for organizations to ensure long-term security, compliance, and operational efficiency. Identity Governance and Administration (IGA) plays a key role in establishing structured policies, enforcing access controls, and managing user identities across complex IT environments. Without a well-defined governance framework, organizations face security risks, regulatory challenges, and inefficiencies that can lead to increased costs and reputational damage. A sustainable governance model provides the foundation for consistent identity management, reducing risks while aligning with business objectives.

The foundation of a sustainable governance model is defining clear roles, responsibilities, and policies for identity and access management. Organizations must establish governance structures that outline who has authority over identity-related decisions, how access is granted and revoked, and what security policies must be enforced. This requires collaboration between IT, security, compliance, and business units to ensure that governance policies align with regulatory requirements and operational needs. A decentralized approach to governance often leads to inconsistencies, while a centralized model provides uniformity and accountability across the organization.

Automation is a critical component of sustainable identity governance. Manual processes for provisioning, de-provisioning, and access certification are inefficient, prone to human error, and difficult to scale. Implementing automated workflows for identity lifecycle management ensures that users receive appropriate access based on business rules while minimizing administrative overhead. Automation also improves compliance by enforcing policies consistently, reducing the likelihood of policy violations and security gaps. By integrating automation with IGA platforms, organizations enhance efficiency while maintaining strong governance controls.

A risk-based approach to governance strengthens sustainability by prioritizing high-risk areas and focusing resources on mitigating threats. Not all access requests and identity-related activities carry the same level of risk, and organizations must tailor their governance models accordingly. Risk scoring mechanisms analyze factors such as user behavior, access history, and privilege levels to determine the potential impact of identity-related risks. By incorporating risk-based access reviews and policy enforcement, businesses can allocate security resources more effectively and prevent unauthorized access before it becomes a threat.

Regulatory compliance is another key driver of governance sustainability. Organizations must navigate a complex landscape of data protection laws, industry regulations, and internal policies. Regulations such as GDPR, HIPAA, and SOX require strict controls over user access, identity management, and data security. A sustainable governance model ensures that compliance is embedded into identity management processes, reducing the burden of manual audits and enforcement. Continuous monitoring, automated compliance reporting, and audit trails provide organizations with the necessary tools to demonstrate adherence to regulatory requirements while reducing the risk of penalties.

Scalability is an essential factor in building a governance model that remains effective as organizations grow. Businesses expand through mergers, acquisitions, and digital transformation initiatives, leading to increasing identity complexity. A governance model that works for a small organization may not be sufficient for a large enterprise with thousands of users and cloud-based applications. Designing governance frameworks with scalability in mind ensures that identity and access policies can be adapted to new business requirements without disrupting operations. Cloud-native IGA solutions and identity federation enable organizations to extend governance controls across hybrid and multi-cloud environments, maintaining consistency across all platforms.

User experience is an often-overlooked aspect of governance sustainability. While security and compliance are top priorities, governance models must also facilitate seamless access to enterprise resources. Employees, contractors, and third-party partners require timely access to applications and data without encountering unnecessary friction. Self-service access management portals, role-based access control (RBAC), and just-in-time access provisioning improve user experience while maintaining security. Striking a balance between security enforcement and usability ensures that governance policies are followed without hindering productivity.

Privileged access management (PAM) is a crucial component of governance models that address high-risk identities. Privileged accounts provide elevated access to critical systems and must be managed with strict controls to prevent misuse or exploitation. Integrating PAM with IGA strengthens governance by enforcing least privilege principles, monitoring privileged sessions, and ensuring that privileged access is granted only when needed. By governing privileged identities with the same rigor as standard user accounts, organizations reduce the risk of insider threats and unauthorized system changes.

Sustainability in governance also depends on continuous improvement and adaptation to emerging threats. Cybersecurity risks evolve rapidly, requiring organizations to update governance policies, access controls, and monitoring capabilities regularly. Identity analytics and artificial intelligence (AI) enhance governance by providing real-time insights into identity risks, detecting anomalies, and recommending policy adjustments. By leveraging AI-driven automation, organizations can proactively adapt governance frameworks to evolving security challenges while maintaining operational resilience.

Governance frameworks must also account for third-party identities, including vendors, suppliers, and external contractors. Third-party users often require access to enterprise systems but pose additional security risks due to lack of direct oversight. A sustainable governance model enforces strict policies for third-party access management, ensuring that external users follow the same security standards as internal employees. Multi-factor authentication (MFA), risk-based access policies, and periodic access reviews help mitigate risks associated with third-party identities while maintaining operational efficiency.

Sustainable governance models rely on a culture of accountability and awareness. Employees and business leaders must understand the importance of identity governance and their role in maintaining security. Security awareness training, policy enforcement, and clear communication of governance expectations help ensure that governance policies are followed consistently. Organizations that foster a security-first mindset reduce the likelihood of policy violations while strengthening their overall governance posture.

A well-structured governance model provides long-term benefits, including reduced security risks, streamlined compliance, and improved operational efficiency. By integrating automation, risk-based policies, and continuous monitoring, organizations can establish a governance framework that adapts to changing business needs and evolving security challenges. Sustainable governance is not a one-time project but an ongoing effort that requires strategic planning, collaboration, and investment in modern identity governance solutions. Businesses that prioritize governance sustainability position themselves for long-term success in managing digital identities and securing enterprise resources.

Best Practices for IGA Implementation

Implementing Identity Governance and Administration (IGA) is essential for organizations seeking to manage digital identities, enforce security policies, and ensure regulatory compliance. As enterprise IT environments become more complex, a well-planned IGA strategy helps streamline identity management, reduce security risks, and improve operational efficiency. Successful implementation requires a structured approach, integrating automation, policy enforcement, and continuous monitoring to maintain effective identity governance.

A key factor in IGA implementation is defining a clear governance framework that aligns with business objectives. Organizations must establish identity management policies that specify who can access what resources, under what conditions, and for how long. Governance frameworks should include role definitions, access approval workflows, and compliance requirements. A well-defined framework ensures consistency across departments while reducing the risk of excessive permissions and unauthorized access.

Automation plays a crucial role in improving efficiency and reducing human error in identity governance. Manual identity and access management processes are time-consuming and prone to misconfigurations that can lead to security breaches. Automating user provisioning, access certification, and de-provisioning ensures that employees receive appropriate access rights when they join the organization and that access is revoked immediately when they leave. Automated workflows also help enforce the principle of least privilege by restricting user access to only what is necessary for their role.

A role-based access control (RBAC) model is a fundamental component of an effective IGA strategy. Organizations should define standard roles based on job functions and assign permissions accordingly. By grouping access privileges into roles, administrators can simplify identity management and reduce the likelihood of privilege creep. In addition to RBAC, organizations should consider implementing policy-based access control (PBAC) to enforce contextual access rules based on factors such as location, device type, and risk level.

Regular access reviews and certification campaigns are critical to maintaining strong identity governance. Over time, employees may accumulate unnecessary access rights, increasing the risk of insider threats or compliance violations. Periodic access reviews allow managers to validate user permissions and remove outdated or excessive access. IGA solutions enable automated access certification workflows, making it easier to conduct reviews and generate audit reports that demonstrate compliance with regulatory requirements.

Privileged access management (PAM) should be integrated with IGA to protect high-risk accounts. Privileged users, such as IT administrators and executives, often have broad access to critical systems and sensitive data. Without proper governance, privileged accounts can become a major security vulnerability. Implementing just-in-time (JIT) access for privileged users, session monitoring, and automated credential rotation enhances security while ensuring that privileged access is granted only when needed.

User experience is an important consideration in IGA implementation. Identity governance should not introduce unnecessary friction for employees, contractors, and business partners. Self-service portals for access requests, password resets, and account management improve efficiency by reducing the workload on IT administrators while empowering users to manage their own identities securely. A well-designed IGA system balances security and usability, ensuring that users can access the resources they need without delays.

Cloud adoption has introduced new challenges for identity governance, requiring organizations to extend IGA policies beyond on-premises systems. Cloud-based applications, SaaS platforms, and multi-cloud environments require consistent identity governance policies to prevent security gaps. IGA solutions must integrate with cloud identity providers, ensuring that cloud access follows the same security controls as on-premises applications. Organizations should also leverage federated identity management and single sign-on (SSO) solutions to simplify authentication across multiple platforms.

Compliance with industry regulations is a driving force behind IGA implementation. Data protection laws such as GDPR, HIPAA, and SOX impose strict requirements on identity governance, requiring organizations to enforce access controls, conduct audits, and generate compliance reports. IGA solutions provide automated compliance tracking, ensuring that organizations can meet regulatory requirements without manual oversight. By maintaining detailed audit logs and implementing access review processes, businesses can reduce compliance risks while improving security posture.

Artificial intelligence and machine learning are transforming IGA by introducing predictive analytics and risk-based decision-making. AI-powered identity analytics detect anomalies in user behavior, flagging suspicious access patterns and recommending corrective actions. Machine learning algorithms can identify trends in access requests, optimize role definitions, and enhance security by dynamically adjusting permissions based on real-time risk assessments. Leveraging AI-driven insights strengthens identity governance while reducing the administrative burden on security teams.

Organizations must also account for third-party access when implementing IGA. Vendors, contractors, and business partners often require temporary access to enterprise systems, but their identities must be governed with the same level of scrutiny as internal users. Implementing strong authentication mechanisms, such as multi-factor authentication (MFA), and enforcing time-limited access controls ensure that third-party users do not retain unnecessary permissions after their engagement ends. Periodic reviews of external user access further reduce security risks associated with third-party accounts.

Zero Trust security principles should be incorporated into IGA strategies to enhance identity governance. Traditional perimeter-based security models are no longer sufficient for protecting modern IT environments, where users access applications from multiple locations and devices. A Zero Trust approach enforces continuous verification of identities, requiring users to authenticate at multiple checkpoints before accessing sensitive resources. Implementing Zero Trust within IGA ensures that access decisions are based on real-time risk analysis rather than static role assignments.

Successful IGA implementation requires continuous monitoring and improvement. Identity governance is not a one-time project but an ongoing process that evolves with organizational changes, security threats, and regulatory updates. Organizations should establish key performance indicators (KPIs) to measure the effectiveness of their IGA programs, such as access review completion rates, time to revoke access for departing employees, and the number of security incidents related to identity misuse. Regular assessments help identify gaps and refine governance strategies to align with evolving business needs.

An effective IGA implementation strategy ensures that identity governance is aligned with business objectives, enhances security, and supports regulatory compliance. By integrating automation, risk-based decision-making, and AI-driven insights, organizations can build a scalable and sustainable IGA framework that protects sensitive data while improving operational efficiency. A well-executed IGA program not only strengthens security but also streamlines identity management processes, allowing businesses to operate with confidence in an increasingly complex digital landscape.

Aligning IGA with Organizational Goals

Identity Governance and Administration (IGA) is a fundamental component of enterprise security, compliance, and operational efficiency. However, for IGA initiatives to be successful, they must align with broader organizational goals rather than operate as isolated IT projects. Effective alignment ensures that identity governance strategies support business objectives, enhance security, and drive digital transformation. Organizations that integrate IGA into their strategic vision can reduce security risks, improve compliance, and streamline access management while fostering innovation and productivity.

One of the primary objectives of any organization is to maintain security and protect sensitive data. Cyber threats continue to evolve, and identity-related breaches remain a leading cause of security incidents. Aligning IGA with security goals helps organizations enforce strong access controls, monitor user activities, and prevent unauthorized access. By implementing role-based access control (RBAC) and policy-based access control (PBAC), organizations can ensure that employees, contractors, and third-party users only have the access they need to perform their tasks. This minimizes the risk of privilege creep and insider threats while supporting a Zero Trust security model.

Regulatory compliance is another critical factor in aligning IGA with business objectives. Many industries are subject to strict regulations, such as GDPR, HIPAA, SOX, and PCI DSS, which require organizations to implement strong identity governance practices. Failure to comply with these regulations can result in financial penalties, reputational damage, and operational disruptions. IGA solutions help organizations meet compliance requirements by automating access reviews, enforcing least privilege policies, and maintaining audit trails. When compliance efforts are integrated into the organization's governance framework, they become proactive rather than reactive, reducing the burden on IT and security teams.

Operational efficiency is a key driver for aligning IGA with organizational goals. Traditional identity management processes often involve manual access provisioning, time-consuming access requests, and inconsistent enforcement of security policies. These inefficiencies can slow down business operations, increase costs, and create frustration for employees. Automating identity lifecycle management through IGA streamlines access provisioning and de-provisioning, reducing administrative overhead while ensuring that users receive timely access to the resources they need. By improving efficiency, IGA allows IT teams to focus on strategic initiatives rather than routine identity management tasks.

Digital transformation initiatives require organizations to adopt new technologies, migrate to cloud environments, and enable remote workforces. As businesses expand their IT ecosystems, identity governance must evolve to support these changes. Aligning IGA with digital transformation goals ensures that organizations can manage identities across hybrid and multi-cloud environments while maintaining security and compliance. IGA solutions integrate with cloud identity providers, enabling organizations to enforce consistent access policies across on-premises and cloud applications. This integration allows for seamless user experiences while maintaining strong governance controls.

Employee productivity is another area where IGA can align with business goals. Organizations that implement self-service access management empower employees to request access to applications and data without unnecessary delays. Automated approval workflows and AI-driven identity analytics enhance decision-making, ensuring that access requests are granted based on business policies rather than manual approvals. This approach reduces downtime, accelerates onboarding processes, and enhances overall workforce efficiency. By providing employees with the tools they need to work securely and efficiently, organizations can improve collaboration and innovation.

Third-party and contractor access management is an often-overlooked aspect of IGA that directly impacts business operations. Many organizations rely on external vendors, consultants, and partners who require access to internal systems. Without proper governance, managing third-party identities can introduce security risks and compliance challenges. Aligning IGA with vendor management processes ensures that third-party users are granted appropriate access levels based on business requirements. Automated provisioning and de-provisioning reduce the risk of orphaned accounts, while continuous monitoring detects potential security threats associated with external identities.

IGA also plays a role in supporting business continuity and risk management strategies. Organizations must be prepared for disruptions caused by cyber incidents, compliance violations, or operational failures. By implementing strong identity governance controls, businesses can quickly respond to security threats, revoke compromised credentials, and enforce emergency access policies. IGA solutions that include real-time monitoring, anomaly detection, and automated remediation help organizations mitigate risks and maintain business continuity during security incidents.

Corporate leadership and executive buy-in are essential for successful IGA implementation. When identity governance is positioned as a strategic business enabler rather than an IT-driven initiative, organizations can secure the necessary resources and support for implementation. Executive sponsorship helps drive cross-functional collaboration between IT, security, compliance, and business units, ensuring that IGA aligns with broader corporate objectives. Communicating the value of IGA in terms of security, compliance, and operational benefits helps stakeholders understand its impact on business success.

Data governance and identity governance often intersect, requiring organizations to align their policies for managing sensitive information. Many business decisions rely on accurate data access and visibility, making it crucial to enforce proper identity controls. By integrating IGA with data governance strategies, organizations can ensure that access to sensitive information is based on business policies and security requirements. This approach reduces data exposure risks while enabling data-driven decision-making processes.

Sustainability and scalability are important considerations for organizations looking to future-proof their identity governance strategies. As businesses grow, their identity environments become more complex, requiring scalable governance frameworks that adapt to evolving needs. Investing in AI-driven identity analytics, automation, and cloud-native IGA solutions ensures that governance remains sustainable over time. Organizations that continuously refine their identity governance practices can maintain alignment with their evolving business goals while staying ahead of emerging security threats.

By embedding IGA into the organization's overall strategic framework, businesses can create a security-first culture that supports growth, innovation, and resilience. Strong identity governance not only enhances security and compliance but also drives efficiency, productivity, and digital transformation. When organizations treat IGA as a critical business function rather than a technical necessity, they can achieve long-term success while minimizing identity-related risks.

Securing Data During Mergers and Acquisitions

Mergers and acquisitions (M&A) present organizations with significant opportunities for growth, market expansion, and operational efficiencies. However, they also introduce complex cybersecurity risks, particularly regarding data security and identity governance. The integration of two companies often involves consolidating IT infrastructures, unifying identity and access management (IAM) systems, and ensuring compliance with regulatory frameworks. Without a structured approach to securing data, organizations face increased risks of data breaches, unauthorized access, and compliance violations. A well-executed Identity Governance and Administration (IGA) strategy plays a critical role in mitigating these risks and ensuring a secure transition during M&A activities.

Data security challenges arise throughout the different phases of an M&A transaction. During the due diligence phase, organizations must assess the security posture of the target company, identify vulnerabilities, and evaluate the potential risks associated with data integration. Companies being acquired may have outdated security controls, inadequate IAM policies, or poor data governance practices that could introduce risks to the acquiring organization. Conducting a comprehensive security assessment, including identity and access audits, helps uncover misconfigurations, excessive permissions, and potential data exposures before the integration process begins.

Once the acquisition is finalized, the next challenge is consolidating and securing user identities. Both organizations typically have separate IAM and IGA systems, leading to overlapping identities, duplicate accounts, and inconsistent access policies. Without proper governance, employees may retain unauthorized access to systems, creating security gaps that attackers can exploit. IGA solutions facilitate identity reconciliation by standardizing access policies, removing redundant accounts, and enforcing least privilege principles. By centralizing identity governance, organizations gain better visibility into who has access to what systems, reducing the risk of insider threats and credential misuse.

Access provisioning and de-provisioning become critical during M&A transitions. Employees from the acquired company may need immediate access to shared systems, cloud applications, and critical business resources. At the same time, certain users may need restricted access as roles are redefined. Automating provisioning processes ensures that access is granted based on business needs while adhering to security policies. Similarly, timely de-provisioning of unnecessary or redundant accounts reduces the attack surface and prevents unauthorized data access.

Privileged access management (PAM) plays a crucial role in securing sensitive data during M&A activities. IT administrators, security teams, and executives from both companies may require temporary privileged access to complete integration tasks, migrate data, and configure security settings. Without proper oversight, privileged accounts become prime targets for cyberattacks and insider threats. Implementing just-in-time (JIT) access and session monitoring ensures that privileged credentials are only used when necessary and are closely tracked for anomalies. Auditing privileged activities helps detect suspicious behavior and strengthens overall security.

Data classification and protection strategies must be aligned between merging entities. Organizations handle various types of sensitive data, including customer information, financial records, intellectual property, and proprietary business data. Differences in data governance policies can create inconsistencies in how sensitive data is stored, shared, and secured. Harmonizing data classification frameworks ensures that critical assets are consistently protected across both organizations. Implementing encryption, access controls, and data loss prevention (DLP) solutions reduces the risk of unauthorized exposure and data leakage.

Regulatory compliance adds another layer of complexity to M&A cybersecurity. Organizations must ensure that data handling practices align with industry-specific regulations such as GDPR, HIPAA, SOX, and PCI DSS. Non-compliance can result in legal penalties, financial losses, and reputational damage. Conducting compliance audits, mapping regulatory obligations across both organizations, and standardizing security policies help maintain compliance throughout the transition. IGA solutions facilitate compliance by automating access certifications, tracking identity changes, and generating audit reports that demonstrate regulatory adherence.

Cloud security integration is another challenge that must be addressed during M&A transitions. Many organizations rely on cloud-based applications and hybrid infrastructures, leading to disparate security models across different cloud providers. Ensuring that identity governance policies extend to cloud platforms, SaaS applications, and multi-cloud environments is essential for securing data. Integrating cloud IAM solutions, enforcing multi-factor authentication (MFA), and implementing federated identity management help maintain a unified security posture.

User training and awareness initiatives support a secure M&A process by reducing the risk of human error. Employees from both organizations must understand new security policies, access protocols, and data protection measures to prevent accidental data exposure or security misconfigurations. Conducting security workshops, providing self-service identity management tools, and reinforcing security best practices empower employees to follow governance policies effectively.

Incident response planning should be a priority during M&A activities. Security incidents such as data breaches, unauthorized access attempts, and phishing attacks often increase during IT transitions. Organizations must establish incident response frameworks that define roles, escalation procedures, and communication protocols in case of security breaches. Real-time monitoring, anomaly detection, and threat intelligence tools provide early warning signs of potential security threats, allowing organizations to respond quickly and mitigate risks.

Zero Trust security principles enhance data protection during M&A processes by enforcing continuous authentication and verification. Instead of assuming trust based on user credentials or network location, Zero Trust ensures that all access requests are verified based on risk assessments, device security posture, and contextual attributes. Applying Zero Trust to identity governance helps prevent unauthorized access while enabling secure collaboration between merging organizations.

A structured post-merger security review ensures that all identity governance policies, access controls, and security measures are fully integrated. Organizations should conduct follow-up security assessments, review audit logs, and validate compliance post-integration. Identifying and remediating security gaps after the merger is completed strengthens the long-term security posture and reduces residual risks. By continuously refining security policies, improving identity governance frameworks, and adapting to evolving cyber threats, organizations can achieve a secure and seamless M&A transition.

Incident Response and Forensic Analysis in IGA

Incident response and forensic analysis play a critical role in Identity Governance and Administration (IGA), ensuring that organizations can detect, investigate, and mitigate security incidents related to identity and access management. As cyber threats become more sophisticated, businesses must be prepared to respond swiftly to identity-based attacks, unauthorized access attempts, and compliance violations. A well-defined incident response strategy, combined with forensic capabilities, strengthens security posture, minimizes the impact of breaches, and helps organizations maintain compliance with regulatory requirements.

Identity-related incidents can take many forms, including unauthorized access, privilege escalation, credential theft, insider threats, and account compromise. A robust incident response plan ensures that security teams can identify suspicious activities, contain threats, and restore normal operations without disruption. Effective response begins with real-time monitoring of identity-related activities, using IGA solutions integrated with Security Information and Event Management (SIEM) systems to analyze authentication logs, access requests, and policy violations.

Detection is the first step in incident response, requiring continuous monitoring of user behavior and access patterns. Anomalous activities, such as repeated failed login attempts, access from unfamiliar locations, or unauthorized privilege escalations, serve as indicators of potential security incidents. Artificial intelligence and machine learning enhance detection capabilities by analyzing behavioral baselines and flagging deviations that suggest malicious intent. When an incident is detected, automated alerts notify security teams, triggering predefined response workflows to mitigate risks before they escalate.

Containment is crucial in preventing security incidents from spreading across an organization's IT infrastructure. Once a suspicious identity-related event is confirmed, immediate action must be taken to limit the attacker's movement. This may involve revoking compromised credentials, disabling affected accounts, enforcing step-up authentication, or temporarily restricting access to sensitive systems. Privileged access management (PAM) solutions play a vital role in containment by ensuring that high-risk accounts are closely monitored and access is restricted based on real-time risk assessments.

Eradication involves eliminating the root cause of the incident, ensuring that attackers can no longer exploit vulnerabilities related to identity governance. This step requires security teams to analyze logs, review access control policies, and close security gaps that allowed the breach to occur. If compromised credentials were involved, password resets and multi-factor authentication (MFA) enforcement are necessary to prevent future unauthorized access. Additionally, organizations must update identity governance policies to strengthen security controls and prevent similar incidents.

Recovery focuses on restoring normal operations while ensuring that security controls remain effective. Organizations must verify that affected identities have been properly remediated and that access privileges are correctly restored without introducing new vulnerabilities. Access review processes help confirm that users retain only the permissions necessary for their roles, preventing privilege creep and ensuring compliance with least privilege principles. Conducting a post-incident review enables organizations to assess response effectiveness and refine security policies based on lessons learned.

Forensic analysis is an essential component of IGA incident response, providing organizations with detailed insights into security events. Digital forensics involves collecting, analyzing, and preserving identity-related data to determine the sequence of events leading up to an incident. IGA solutions provide comprehensive audit logs that track user activities, access modifications, and authentication attempts, enabling forensic investigators to reconstruct attack timelines and identify the tactics, techniques, and procedures (TTPs) used by adversaries.

Log analysis plays a crucial role in forensic investigations, helping security teams identify patterns of unauthorized access and privilege abuse. By correlating IGA logs with SIEM data, organizations gain a deeper understanding of how attackers navigated through systems, which accounts were compromised, and what data may have been exposed. Advanced identity analytics enhance forensic capabilities by detecting hidden threats, identifying previously undetected access anomalies, and providing contextual risk assessments.

Regulatory compliance requires organizations to maintain detailed records of security incidents and forensic investigations. Regulations such as GDPR, HIPAA, and SOX mandate strict identity governance controls and audit reporting, requiring businesses to demonstrate how they detect, respond to, and mitigate identity-related threats. IGA solutions facilitate compliance by automating incident documentation, generating forensic reports, and ensuring that access review processes align with regulatory standards. Organizations must retain forensic data for extended periods to support legal investigations and compliance audits.

Proactive measures, such as regular penetration testing and red team exercises, strengthen incident response and forensic capabilities by simulating real-world attacks. These assessments help organizations identify weaknesses in identity governance frameworks, test detection and response mechanisms, and refine security policies. By continuously evaluating IGA security posture, businesses can enhance their ability to respond to emerging threats and reduce incident response times.

Collaboration between security teams, IT administrators, and compliance officers is essential for effective incident response and forensic analysis in IGA. Establishing clear communication channels, defining escalation procedures, and conducting regular incident response training ensures that stakeholders are prepared to respond to identity-related incidents. Cross-functional collaboration enhances security awareness, fosters a culture of accountability, and improves overall incident handling efficiency.

As identity-based attacks become more frequent and sophisticated, organizations must adopt a proactive approach to incident response and forensic analysis. Implementing advanced detection capabilities, automating response workflows, and leveraging forensic insights enable businesses to strengthen their identity governance frameworks and protect critical assets. By continuously refining incident response strategies and forensic investigation processes, organizations can minimize the impact of security incidents and build a resilient identity security posture.

Case Studies: Successful IGA Deployments

Identity Governance and Administration (IGA) is a cornerstone of modern security frameworks, enabling organizations to manage digital identities, enforce access policies, and ensure compliance with regulatory requirements. Successful IGA deployments provide real-world examples of how enterprises across various industries have strengthened security, improved efficiency, and minimized identity-related risks. These case studies illustrate the impact of well-executed IGA implementations, highlighting best practices, challenges, and outcomes.

A leading global financial institution faced significant challenges in managing employee access to critical banking applications. The organization relied on manual access provisioning and certification processes, leading to delays, compliance risks, and audit deficiencies. With financial regulations such as SOX and PCI DSS requiring strict access controls, the bank needed a solution to automate identity management, reduce human error, and improve security oversight.

The implementation of an enterprise-wide IGA solution automated the provisioning and de-provisioning of user accounts based on job roles and business policies. Role-based access control (RBAC) ensured that employees received only the necessary permissions, preventing excessive privileges and unauthorized access. Automated access certification workflows enabled managers to conduct periodic reviews efficiently, ensuring that all access rights remained justified and compliant. By integrating IGA with the organization's HR system, user onboarding and offboarding became seamless, reducing the time required to grant or revoke access from days to minutes. The result was a 70% reduction in manual access-related tasks, enhanced regulatory compliance, and a significant decrease in audit findings related to identity management.

In the healthcare industry, a large hospital network struggled with managing access for thousands of doctors, nurses, and administrative staff across multiple facilities. The complexity of maintaining secure access to electronic health records (EHR), medical devices, and cloud applications posed a serious risk to patient data security. Compliance with HIPAA regulations required strict identity governance controls to prevent unauthorized access to sensitive medical information.

To address these challenges, the hospital deployed a centralized IGA solution that provided automated identity lifecycle management, real-time access monitoring, and fine-grained permission controls. The implementation included the use of multi-factor authentication (MFA) for high-risk applications and automated role assignments based on job functions. Doctors and nurses received just-in-time access to patient records based on their shift schedules, reducing unnecessary exposure to sensitive data. The IGA system also enabled real-time access revocation when staff members left the organization or changed roles, ensuring that former employees could no longer access confidential patient data. Post-implementation results showed a 60% improvement in compliance audit scores, reduced insider threat risks, and improved user efficiency by eliminating redundant access request approvals.

A multinational manufacturing company with operations across multiple countries faced difficulties in managing third-party access. The company relied on numerous vendors, suppliers, and contractors who required temporary access to internal systems, but tracking and revoking their access was inconsistent. As a result, dormant and orphaned accounts remained active long after vendor contracts expired, creating significant security vulnerabilities.

The organization implemented an IGA solution with a strong focus on third-party identity governance. The new system introduced automated workflows for granting temporary access with predefined expiration dates. When vendor contracts ended, access was automatically revoked unless explicitly renewed through an approval process. Additionally, the solution incorporated AI-driven risk analytics to monitor third-party access behaviors, flagging any suspicious activities. By deploying a centralized identity governance framework, the company reduced security risks associated with external users by 80% and streamlined third-party access reviews, cutting administrative overhead by half.

A government agency responsible for handling citizen data encountered persistent issues with identity reconciliation and compliance enforcement. Different departments operated independent identity management systems, leading to duplicated accounts, inconsistent access policies, and regulatory non-compliance. The fragmented approach made it difficult to enforce least privilege access and conduct effective audits.

To unify identity governance across all departments, the agency deployed an IGA solution that consolidated identity records, standardized access policies, and enforced consistent security controls. AI-driven identity analytics helped detect redundant or conflicting user permissions, ensuring that access rights adhered to policy guidelines. Automated compliance reporting simplified the audit process, reducing the time required for regulatory reporting by 50%. The agency also implemented privileged access management (PAM) controls to secure administrative accounts, preventing unauthorized system modifications. As a result, compliance violations dropped significantly, and the agency achieved a more transparent and secure identity management structure.

A large retail organization undergoing rapid digital transformation faced challenges securing employee access to a growing number of cloud applications. The traditional on-premises identity management system lacked integration with cloud-based services, leading to inefficient user provisioning and increased security gaps. Employees frequently struggled with multiple login credentials, resulting in poor user experience and higher IT support costs.

By deploying a cloud-native IGA solution, the retailer was able to integrate identity governance across both on-premises and cloud applications. Single sign-on (SSO) and federated identity management reduced login complexities, improving employee productivity and reducing helpdesk requests related to password resets by 40%. Automated access policies ensured that users received the correct permissions for cloud applications, and real-time monitoring provided visibility into access activities. The retailer also implemented conditional access policies, restricting access to critical applications based on user risk profiles and behavioral analytics. Post-implementation benefits included improved security, faster user onboarding, and greater operational efficiency in managing cloud-based identities.

Each of these case studies demonstrates the transformative impact of IGA when aligned with organizational needs. By leveraging automation, enforcing role-based policies, and integrating AI-driven insights, organizations across industries have strengthened security, enhanced compliance, and optimized identity management processes. A strategic approach to IGA implementation not only mitigates identity-related risks but also improves overall business agility and efficiency in an evolving digital landscape.

IGA in Financial Services

Identity Governance and Administration (IGA) is a critical component of security and regulatory compliance in the financial services sector. Financial institutions manage large volumes of sensitive data, including customer records, transaction details, and financial assets. With increasing cyber threats, stringent regulatory requirements, and complex IT environments, effective identity governance ensures that only authorized individuals have access to critical systems, mitigating risks associated with unauthorized access, fraud, and data breaches. A well-implemented IGA strategy enhances security, streamlines compliance, and improves operational efficiency in financial organizations.

Regulatory compliance is a primary driver for IGA adoption in financial services. Institutions must comply with industry regulations such as the Sarbanes-Oxley Act (SOX), the Gramm-Leach-Bliley Act (GLBA), the Payment Card Industry Data Security Standard (PCI DSS), and the European Union's General Data Protection Regulation (GDPR). These regulations require strict controls over user identities, access privileges, and audit reporting. IGA solutions help financial organizations enforce compliance by automating access reviews, maintaining audit logs, and ensuring that identity management policies align with regulatory mandates.

Access control and least privilege enforcement are essential for securing financial data. Employees, contractors, and third-party vendors require access to various banking systems, payment platforms, and financial applications. Without proper governance, users may accumulate excessive privileges over time, leading to an increased risk of fraud or insider threats. Role-based access control (RBAC) and policy-based access control (PBAC) mechanisms help financial institutions grant appropriate permissions based on job functions while preventing unauthorized access. Automated provisioning and de-provisioning processes ensure that access rights are assigned and revoked in real time, reducing the likelihood of lingering or orphaned accounts.

Privileged access management (PAM) plays a crucial role in financial IGA frameworks. Privileged users, such as system administrators and financial executives, often have elevated permissions that grant access to critical infrastructure and transaction processing systems. Cybercriminals frequently target privileged accounts to execute fraudulent transactions or disrupt financial operations. Integrating PAM with IGA solutions enables organizations to enforce just-in-time access, implement multi-factor authentication (MFA), and monitor privileged sessions in real time. This approach minimizes the attack surface while ensuring that privileged access is granted only when necessary.

Fraud prevention and risk management are key considerations in financial services. Identity-based fraud, including account takeovers, insider trading, and unauthorized fund transfers, pose significant threats to institutions and their customers. AI-driven identity analytics enhance IGA by detecting anomalies in user behavior, flagging suspicious transactions, and identifying deviations from normal access patterns. Continuous monitoring and real-time risk scoring enable financial organizations to respond proactively to potential security incidents before they escalate into full-scale breaches.

Third-party and vendor access management require strict governance controls in financial institutions. Many organizations rely on external service providers, consultants, and software vendors who need access to banking systems and customer databases. Without a structured approach to managing third-party identities, financial institutions risk exposing sensitive data to unauthorized parties. Enforcing strict onboarding processes, conducting periodic access reviews, and implementing time-restricted access policies help mitigate risks associated with external users. Identity federation and single sign-on (SSO) solutions further enhance security by ensuring that third-party access follows the same governance standards as internal employees.

Cloud adoption in financial services introduces additional identity governance challenges. Many institutions are transitioning to cloud-based core banking systems, digital payment platforms, and financial analytics tools. Managing identities across on-premises and cloud environments requires a unified governance approach to ensure consistent access policies, security controls, and compliance reporting. IGA solutions that integrate with cloud identity providers enable seamless identity synchronization, centralized access management, and automated enforcement of cloud security policies.

Customer identity and access management (CIAM) is another critical aspect of IGA in financial services. Banks and financial institutions must provide secure, seamless access to digital banking services while protecting customer data from fraud and identity theft. Implementing strong authentication mechanisms, such as biometric verification and adaptive authentication, helps prevent unauthorized access. IGA solutions enhance CIAM by ensuring that customer identities are managed securely, access requests are validated, and fraudulent activities are detected early.

Incident response and breach mitigation rely on effective identity governance. Financial institutions must be prepared to respond to identity-related security incidents, such as credential compromise or privilege abuse. A well-structured IGA framework enables rapid response by automatically revoking access to compromised accounts, enforcing step-up authentication for high-risk transactions, and generating detailed audit logs for forensic investigations. Automated remediation workflows reduce incident response times while minimizing financial and reputational damage.

IGA also supports digital transformation initiatives in financial services. As institutions embrace artificial intelligence, blockchain, and fintech integrations, identity governance ensures that new technologies align with security and compliance requirements. Automated identity lifecycle management simplifies onboarding and offboarding processes, allowing financial organizations to scale efficiently while maintaining security best practices. By embedding IGA into digital innovation strategies, financial institutions can enhance customer trust, streamline operations, and reduce identity-related risks.

A proactive approach to IGA strengthens security, regulatory compliance, and operational efficiency in financial services. By integrating automation, AI-driven identity analytics, and strict access controls, financial institutions can protect sensitive data, prevent fraud, and maintain compliance with evolving regulations. Identity governance remains a cornerstone of financial cybersecurity, enabling organizations to navigate digital transformation while safeguarding their most valuable assets.

IGA in Healthcare and Pharmaceuticals

Identity Governance and Administration (IGA) is a critical component of security and compliance in the healthcare and pharmaceutical industries. Organizations in these sectors handle vast amounts of sensitive data, including patient records, clinical research, drug formulations, and intellectual property. The need for robust identity governance arises from the complexity of managing access for healthcare professionals, researchers, administrative staff, and third-party vendors while ensuring compliance with strict regulatory requirements. Effective IGA implementation strengthens security, improves operational efficiency, and supports compliance with regulations such as HIPAA, GDPR, and FDA 21 CFR Part 11.

The healthcare industry faces unique challenges in identity and access management due to its highly dynamic workforce. Doctors, nurses, and specialists often work across multiple locations, requiring rapid access to electronic health records (EHRs) and medical applications. At the same time, temporary workers, visiting physicians, and external consultants need controlled access to critical systems. Without a strong IGA framework, managing these access requirements manually becomes inefficient and increases the risk of unauthorized access to patient data. Automating identity lifecycle management ensures that users receive the right level of access based on their roles and that access is revoked immediately when no longer needed.

Role-based access control (RBAC) and policy-based access control (PBAC) help healthcare organizations enforce least privilege principles. By defining access policies based on job roles, institutions can ensure that only authorized personnel can view or modify patient records, prescribe medications, or access laboratory systems. Policy-based access further enhances security by incorporating contextual factors such as location, device type, and authentication strength. For example, a doctor accessing an EHR system from a hospital network may receive full access, while the same request from an external device may trigger additional authentication requirements or restrict certain actions.

Privileged access management (PAM) plays a crucial role in securing highly sensitive data in healthcare and pharmaceutical organizations. Administrative accounts with elevated privileges pose significant security risks if mismanaged or compromised. PAM solutions integrated with IGA ensure that privileged access is granted only when necessary and that all activities are logged for auditing purposes. Just-in-time (JIT) access controls further reduce the risk of privilege misuse by limiting the duration of administrative access to critical systems.

The pharmaceutical sector relies on identity governance to protect intellectual property, clinical trial data, and supply chain systems. Research and development (R&D) teams require access to proprietary drug research and experimental data, making access control a high-priority security concern. Collaboration between multiple stakeholders, including external research partners, contract manufacturers, and regulatory bodies, introduces additional identity governance challenges. IGA solutions streamline external access management by enforcing strict authentication controls, ensuring data segmentation, and applying access policies that align with regulatory standards.

Regulatory compliance is a driving factor for IGA adoption in healthcare and pharmaceuticals. The Health Insurance Portability and Accountability Act (HIPAA) mandates strict access controls and audit trails to protect patient health information (PHI). Organizations must demonstrate that they enforce access policies, conduct regular reviews, and maintain detailed records of who accessed sensitive data. IGA solutions automate compliance tracking, generate audit-ready reports, and provide continuous monitoring to detect unauthorized access attempts. Similarly, pharmaceutical companies must comply with FDA regulations, such as 21 CFR Part 11, which requires secure identity verification and electronic record-keeping for clinical trials and drug approvals.

Identity reconciliation is essential for large healthcare networks and pharmaceutical enterprises that operate across multiple facilities and IT systems. Many organizations have fragmented identity repositories, with separate access management systems for hospitals, research centers, manufacturing plants, and corporate offices. This fragmentation leads to inconsistencies in identity governance, orphaned accounts, and potential security gaps. IGA solutions integrate with existing identity stores, providing centralized visibility and enforcing uniform access policies across all business units.

Third-party access management is another critical consideration for healthcare and pharmaceutical organizations. External contractors, research partners, and IT vendors frequently require temporary access to critical systems. Without proper governance, third-party users may retain access longer than necessary, increasing the risk of security breaches. Implementing automated workflows for third-party identity lifecycle management ensures that access is provisioned based on contracts and automatically revoked upon expiration. Continuous monitoring and AI-driven risk analysis further enhance security by detecting anomalous access patterns associated with external identities.

The increasing adoption of cloud-based healthcare applications introduces new identity governance challenges. Organizations must ensure that cloud services adhere to the same security and compliance standards as on-premises systems. Federated identity management enables seamless single sign-on (SSO) across cloud platforms while maintaining centralized governance policies. Multi-factor authentication (MFA) strengthens cloud security by requiring additional verification before granting access to sensitive applications. By extending IGA to cloud environments, healthcare and pharmaceutical organizations maintain security consistency while enabling digital transformation initiatives.

Data privacy and security risks continue to evolve, requiring proactive identity governance measures. Cyberattacks targeting healthcare institutions and pharmaceutical companies have increased, with ransomware, phishing, and credential theft posing significant threats. AI-driven identity analytics enhance IGA by detecting unusual access behaviors, flagging potential insider threats, and automating response actions. Real-time anomaly detection helps prevent data breaches by identifying and mitigating suspicious identity activities before they escalate.

IGA also plays a role in improving operational efficiency by reducing administrative overhead. Manual access request approvals, employee onboarding delays, and inefficient access reviews can slow down productivity and impact patient care. Automating these processes allows healthcare professionals and researchers to focus on their core responsibilities while ensuring that security policies are consistently enforced. Self-service identity management portals further improve efficiency by enabling users to request access, reset passwords, and update credentials without IT intervention.

As healthcare and pharmaceutical organizations continue to adopt digital technologies, the need for a robust IGA framework becomes increasingly vital. A well-implemented IGA strategy ensures that access to sensitive data is controlled, monitored, and aligned with compliance requirements. By leveraging automation, AI-driven analytics, and policy-based access controls, organizations can strengthen security, enhance compliance, and improve operational efficiency.

IGA in Education and Research Institutions

Identity Governance and Administration (IGA) plays a crucial role in education and research institutions, where managing user identities, access privileges, and compliance requirements is increasingly complex. Universities, colleges, and research centers operate in highly dynamic environments where students, faculty, staff, and external collaborators require secure access to various systems, including learning management platforms, administrative databases, and research networks. Without effective identity governance, institutions face challenges related to unauthorized access, data security, and compliance with regulations such as FERPA, GDPR, and HIPAA. Implementing a robust IGA framework enhances security, streamlines user management, and supports academic and research objectives.

Higher education institutions handle a constantly changing user base, as students enroll, graduate, and transfer, while faculty and researchers frequently move between departments and institutions. This dynamic nature makes identity lifecycle management a fundamental aspect of IGA. Automating user provisioning and de-provisioning ensures that individuals receive the correct access when they join and lose access when they leave. Without automated identity lifecycle management, institutions risk leaving orphaned accounts active, creating security vulnerabilities and potential breaches.

Role-based access control (RBAC) and policy-based access control (PBAC) are essential for maintaining security and efficiency in educational institutions. Different users require access to various systems, such as students needing access to course materials, faculty requiring administrative privileges, and researchers requiring specialized computing resources. Implementing RBAC ensures that access permissions align with academic roles, while PBAC enables more granular control based on contextual factors such as location, device type, and authentication strength. These governance models help prevent privilege creep, ensuring that users only have access to the resources necessary for their roles.

Research institutions face additional challenges in identity governance due to the need for secure collaboration with external researchers, industry partners, and funding agencies. Many research projects involve sensitive data, including proprietary intellectual property, medical research data, and classified government-funded projects. IGA frameworks help manage external identities by enforcing strict authentication measures, ensuring that only authorized individuals can access sensitive research information. Multi-factor authentication

(MFA), federated identity management, and just-in-time access provisioning enhance security while allowing seamless collaboration across institutions.

Third-party and guest access management is another critical aspect of IGA in education. Universities frequently host visiting scholars, guest lecturers, and external consultants who require temporary access to academic and research systems. Without a structured governance framework, these temporary users may retain access long after their association with the institution ends. Implementing automated workflows for third-party identity lifecycle management ensures that temporary accounts are created with predefined expiration dates and that access is revoked automatically when no longer required.

Cloud adoption has become prevalent in higher education, with institutions leveraging cloud-based learning platforms, collaboration tools, and research infrastructures. Managing identities across on-premises and cloud environments requires a unified governance approach to enforce consistent access policies and security controls. Integrating IGA with cloud identity providers enables seamless identity synchronization, centralizes user access management, and improves visibility into authentication activities across multiple platforms. Cloud-based IGA solutions help institutions maintain control over distributed identities while supporting digital transformation initiatives.

Compliance with regulatory frameworks is a major concern for educational and research institutions. The Family Educational Rights and Privacy Act (FERPA) in the United States mandates strict controls over student records, requiring institutions to protect access to personal data. In Europe, the General Data Protection Regulation (GDPR) imposes stringent data privacy requirements, making it essential for universities to implement access governance controls that limit data exposure. Additionally, research institutions handling medical data must comply with the Health Insurance Portability and Accountability Act (HIPAA), which enforces strict security measures for health-related information. IGA solutions assist institutions in maintaining compliance by enforcing access policies, automating audit reporting, and ensuring that user activities are logged and reviewed regularly.

Privileged access management (PAM) is vital for securing administrative and research systems in higher education. IT administrators, database managers, and faculty members with elevated privileges pose security risks if their credentials are compromised. Cyberattacks targeting universities and research institutions have increased, with ransomware attacks and credential theft posing serious threats. Implementing PAM alongside IGA frameworks ensures that privileged accounts are closely monitored, access is granted only when necessary, and high-risk activities are logged and reviewed.

User experience is an important consideration in IGA implementation for education and research institutions. While security is a top priority, students and faculty members require easy access to academic resources. Implementing single sign-on (SSO) and federated identity management reduces login friction by allowing users to authenticate once and gain access to multiple applications. This approach improves convenience while maintaining strong identity governance controls. Self-service identity management portals further enhance user experience by enabling students and faculty to manage their access requests, reset passwords, and update account details without IT intervention.

Identity governance also supports diversity in learning models, including remote education, hybrid classrooms, and international research collaborations. As institutions expand their digital presence, securing remote access to learning platforms and research data becomes essential. Adaptive authentication mechanisms, risk-based access controls, and continuous monitoring help institutions balance security and accessibility. AI-driven identity analytics can detect anomalies in user behavior, identifying potential security threats and automatically adjusting access policies based on risk assessments.

Research funding agencies and government institutions often impose strict cybersecurity requirements on universities conducting funded research. Implementing a robust IGA framework helps institutions demonstrate compliance with funding agency security mandates, reducing the risk of losing grants due to inadequate security practices. Automated compliance tracking and audit capabilities provide institutions with the ability to generate reports demonstrating adherence to access control policies and security best practices.

Higher education institutions that invest in IGA frameworks benefit from enhanced security, streamlined identity management, and improved compliance. By leveraging automation, role-based policies, and AI-driven insights, universities and research centers can manage digital identities more effectively, reducing risks associated with unauthorized access and data breaches. As academic institutions continue to embrace digital learning and global research collaborations, a strong identity governance strategy remains essential for maintaining security and operational efficiency.

IGA in Government and Public Sector

Identity Governance and Administration (IGA) is a crucial component of cybersecurity and regulatory compliance in the government and public sector. Agencies and public institutions manage vast amounts of sensitive data, including citizen records, national security information, law enforcement data, and critical infrastructure systems. Ensuring proper access control while maintaining operational efficiency requires a strong identity governance framework. With growing cyber threats, evolving regulatory mandates, and the increasing adoption of digital services, governments must implement effective IGA solutions to secure identities, enforce policies, and maintain transparency.

Government agencies face unique challenges in identity governance due to the size and complexity of their operations. Unlike private enterprises, public sector organizations must manage identities across multiple departments, agencies, and jurisdictions. Employees, contractors, law enforcement personnel, and public officials require access to various systems, ranging from tax databases to social services applications. Without a centralized governance model, agencies risk mismanaging user identities, leading to security vulnerabilities and operational inefficiencies. A well-implemented IGA solution provides a unified approach to identity management, ensuring that access policies are consistently applied across all government entities.

Regulatory compliance is a significant driver of IGA adoption in the public sector. Government institutions must adhere to strict security and data protection standards, including regulations such as the General Data Protection Regulation (GDPR), the Federal Information Security Management Act (FISMA), and the National Institute of Standards and Technology (NIST) cybersecurity framework. These regulations require agencies to enforce strong access controls, conduct regular audits, and ensure accountability for identity-related activities. IGA solutions help automate compliance tracking by providing audit logs, access review mechanisms, and policy enforcement tools that align with regulatory requirements.

Access control in government agencies must balance security with accessibility. Employees and public officials need timely access to data and applications to perform their duties efficiently, while unauthorized access must be prevented. Role-based access control (RBAC) and policy-based access control (PBAC) provide a structured approach to managing user permissions. By defining access roles based on job functions, agencies can prevent privilege creep and reduce the risk of unauthorized data exposure. Policy-driven access models further enhance security by incorporating contextual factors such as device security posture, location, and time of access.

Privileged access management (PAM) is especially critical in the government sector, where administrative users have access to highly sensitive systems. Cybercriminals and nation-state actors often target privileged accounts to gain control of critical infrastructure, financial systems, and classified information. Implementing PAM solutions alongside IGA ensures that privileged users follow strict authentication protocols, session monitoring, and just-in-time access policies. By reducing the attack surface for privileged accounts, government institutions strengthen their security posture and minimize insider threats.

Third-party identity governance is another crucial aspect of IGA in the public sector. Government agencies frequently collaborate with external contractors, vendors, and service providers who require temporary access to secure systems. Without proper identity governance, third-party users may retain access beyond their contract period, increasing the risk of security breaches. Implementing automated provisioning and de-provisioning workflows ensures that third-party access is granted based on contract terms and is automatically revoked when no longer needed. Continuous monitoring and periodic access reviews further enhance security by ensuring that external identities do not pose a risk to government systems.

As digital transformation accelerates, government agencies are increasingly adopting cloud-based applications and hybrid IT environments. Managing identities across on-premises systems and cloud services requires a modernized IGA strategy that integrates cloud identity providers and federated authentication mechanisms. Cloud-based IGA solutions enable agencies to enforce consistent access policies across all environments while maintaining centralized visibility into identity-related activities. Multi-factor authentication (MFA) and single sign-on (SSO) solutions further enhance security by reducing reliance on passwords and ensuring secure authentication for government employees and public users.

Citizen identity management presents additional challenges in the public sector. Government agencies are responsible for verifying and managing the identities of millions of citizens for services such as healthcare, taxation, and social benefits. Ensuring that only authorized individuals access government services while protecting citizen data from fraud and identity theft requires a robust IGA framework. Implementing self-service identity verification, biometric authentication, and risk-based access controls improves the security and efficiency of digital public services. AI-driven identity analytics help detect anomalies in citizen account activity, preventing fraudulent access to government programs.

Incident response and risk mitigation are integral to IGA in government institutions. Cyberattacks targeting government agencies are on the rise, with threat actors attempting to exploit weak identity controls to gain access to classified information and disrupt critical services. A well-defined incident response plan ensures that security teams can quickly detect and contain identity-related security breaches. IGA solutions provide real-time monitoring, automated threat detection, and forensic analysis capabilities, enabling agencies to investigate and respond to security incidents effectively. Implementing identity-based risk scoring further strengthens security by continuously assessing user behavior and adjusting access controls based on risk levels.

Data sovereignty and national security concerns also influence IGA strategies in the public sector. Governments must ensure that sensitive data is stored, processed, and accessed in compliance with national security policies and jurisdictional regulations. Implementing geo-fencing policies, enforcing data residency requirements, and restricting access based on user location help prevent unauthorized cross-border data transfers. By integrating identity governance with national security frameworks, government agencies can safeguard critical data assets while maintaining compliance with sovereign data protection laws.

IGA also plays a role in modernizing legacy systems within government institutions. Many agencies still rely on outdated identity management processes that lack automation, scalability, and integration capabilities. Transitioning to an IGA framework modernizes identity governance by streamlining administrative processes, reducing manual access provisioning, and improving visibility into user access patterns. AI-driven automation reduces the burden on IT administrators while enhancing the accuracy and efficiency of identity governance processes.

Public trust in government institutions depends on the security and transparency of identity management practices. Ensuring that access to government data and services is controlled, monitored, and accountable enhances citizen confidence in digital governance initiatives. By adopting advanced IGA solutions, government agencies can create a secure and efficient identity governance framework that supports public sector innovation, protects sensitive information, and enables the seamless delivery of digital services.

IGA for Small and Medium Enterprises (SMEs)

Identity Governance and Administration (IGA) is often associated with large enterprises, but small and medium enterprises (SMEs) also face significant security and compliance challenges that necessitate a robust identity governance strategy. As SMEs increasingly adopt cloud services, remote work, and digital transformation initiatives, managing user identities, access controls, and compliance obligations becomes critical. Without proper identity governance, SMEs risk unauthorized access, data breaches, and regulatory penalties that can have severe financial and reputational consequences. Implementing an effective IGA framework enables SMEs to enhance security, improve operational efficiency, and ensure compliance while maintaining cost-effectiveness.

SMEs operate with lean IT teams that often manage multiple responsibilities, making automation a key component of IGA. Unlike large enterprises with dedicated identity management teams, SMEs benefit from automated provisioning and de-provisioning of user accounts, reducing administrative burdens and minimizing human error. When employees join, change roles, or leave the organization, an automated IGA solution ensures that they are granted appropriate access rights and that unnecessary privileges are revoked promptly. This prevents unauthorized access to critical systems and reduces security vulnerabilities associated with orphaned accounts.

Role-based access control (RBAC) and policy-based access control (PBAC) provide SMEs with structured identity governance, ensuring that employees have access only to the systems necessary for their roles. In smaller organizations, where employees may wear multiple hats, it is common for access permissions to expand over time, leading to privilege creep. Implementing access policies based on job functions prevents excessive permissions, mitigating insider threats and reducing the risk of accidental or intentional data misuse. By enforcing least privilege access, SMEs create a security-first culture that aligns with best practices in identity governance.

Cybersecurity threats pose a growing risk to SMEs, as attackers often target smaller businesses due to perceived weaker security defenses. Credential theft, phishing attacks, and unauthorized access are common threats that exploit poorly managed identities. IGA solutions with multi-factor authentication (MFA) and risk-based authentication strengthen security by requiring additional verification for high-risk access attempts. AI-driven identity analytics further enhance security by detecting anomalies in user behavior, flagging suspicious login attempts, and providing real-time risk assessments that enable proactive threat mitigation.

Third-party access management is another essential aspect of IGA for SMEs, as many organizations rely on external vendors, contractors, and freelancers for IT support, marketing, and operations. Without a proper governance framework, managing third-party access can lead to security risks, particularly if temporary users retain access beyond the required timeframe. Automated workflows that provision access based on contract terms and revoke permissions upon project completion help SMEs maintain control over external identities. Continuous monitoring of third-party activities ensures that access remains appropriate and secure.

Cloud adoption among SMEs has increased significantly, with businesses leveraging software-as-a-service (SaaS) applications, cloud storage, and remote collaboration tools. While cloud services improve flexibility and scalability, they also introduce identity governance challenges. Many SMEs struggle with managing multiple cloud identities across different platforms, leading to inconsistent access controls and security gaps. Integrating IGA solutions with cloud identity providers centralizes identity management, ensuring that access policies are consistently enforced across all environments. Single sign-on (SSO) and federated identity management simplify authentication processes while maintaining strong governance controls.

Regulatory compliance is becoming a growing concern for SMEs, as data protection laws such as GDPR, HIPAA, and PCI DSS apply to businesses of all sizes. Failure to comply with these regulations can result in legal penalties, data breaches, and reputational damage. IGA solutions help SMEs meet compliance requirements by enforcing access policies, automating audit reporting, and providing visibility into user activities. Periodic access reviews ensure that only authorized users retain access to sensitive information, reducing the risk of non-compliance. By integrating IGA with compliance frameworks, SMEs can streamline audit preparation and demonstrate adherence to regulatory standards.

Cost-effectiveness is a major factor for SMEs considering IGA implementation. Unlike large enterprises with substantial IT budgets, SMEs require scalable solutions that provide security without excessive costs. Cloud-based IGA solutions offer a cost-effective approach, eliminating the need for expensive on-premises infrastructure while providing enterprise-grade security features. Many IGA vendors offer subscription-based pricing models, allowing SMEs to pay for only the features they need. Investing in identity governance not only reduces security risks but also improves operational efficiency by automating manual processes and reducing IT workload.

User experience plays an important role in IGA adoption for SMEs, as employees expect seamless access to applications and data without unnecessary friction. Self-service portals for password resets, access requests, and role management empower employees to manage their identities independently, reducing reliance on IT support. SSO solutions further enhance user experience by eliminating the need for multiple passwords while improving security through centralized authentication. A well-implemented IGA strategy balances security and convenience, enabling SMEs to operate efficiently without compromising identity governance.

Business continuity and risk management are strengthened through effective identity governance. SMEs that experience cyber incidents, employee turnover, or operational disruptions must ensure that access to critical systems remains secure. An IGA framework that includes real-time access monitoring, automated incident response, and forensic audit capabilities enables organizations to detect and respond to identity-related threats quickly. By implementing identity governance as a proactive security measure, SMEs reduce their exposure to cyber risks and enhance resilience in the face of evolving threats.

As digital transformation accelerates, SMEs must recognize the importance of IGA in safeguarding their business operations. Implementing a scalable and automated identity governance framework provides long-term benefits, including reduced security risks, improved compliance, and streamlined identity management. By leveraging cloud-based IGA solutions, enforcing role-based access controls, and integrating AI-driven analytics, SMEs can achieve enterprise-level security without overwhelming their IT resources. Identity governance is no longer a luxury reserved for large corporations but a necessity for businesses of all sizes looking to protect their data, employees, and reputation.

Emerging Trends in IGA

Identity Governance and Administration (IGA) is evolving rapidly to meet the challenges of digital transformation, hybrid work environments, cloud adoption, and increasing cyber threats. Organizations are shifting from traditional identity management approaches to more dynamic, AI-driven, and risk-based strategies that enhance security, improve efficiency, and ensure compliance. Several emerging trends in IGA are reshaping how businesses manage identities, enforce access policies, and mitigate identity-related risks.

One of the most significant trends in IGA is the integration of artificial intelligence (AI) and machine learning (ML) to improve identity analytics and automate decision-making. AI-driven identity governance solutions can analyze user behavior, detect anomalies, and provide risk-based recommendations for access provisioning and de-provisioning. Machine learning algorithms help identify patterns that indicate privilege misuse, insider threats, or potential security breaches, allowing organizations to take proactive security measures. AI also enhances role mining and optimization by analyzing historical access patterns to recommend efficient role structures that align with business needs.

Another critical development in IGA is the adoption of Zero Trust principles. Organizations are moving away from traditional perimeter-based security models to a framework where every access request is continuously verified. Zero Trust IGA enforces least privilege access by dynamically adjusting permissions based on real-time risk assessments. Multi-factor authentication (MFA), continuous access reviews, and adaptive authentication mechanisms are becoming standard practices to ensure that users have only the necessary access at any given time. By implementing Zero Trust, businesses strengthen identity governance by eliminating implicit trust and verifying each identity, device, and request independently.

The rise of hybrid and multi-cloud environments has introduced new challenges in identity governance, driving the need for unified IGA solutions. Organizations are no longer operating within a single IT infrastructure; instead, they use a combination of on-premises systems, cloud-based applications, and SaaS platforms. Managing identities across multiple environments requires a centralized governance model that enforces consistent security policies and access controls. Cloud-native IGA solutions are gaining traction, offering seamless integration with cloud identity providers and providing visibility into user activities across diverse ecosystems.

The increasing complexity of identity ecosystems has also led to the adoption of identity automation and orchestration. Organizations are leveraging robotic process automation (RPA) and workflow automation to streamline identity lifecycle management. Automated provisioning and de-provisioning ensure that users receive the correct access based on business rules, reducing the administrative burden on IT teams. Orchestration tools enable organizations to create automated workflows for role approvals, compliance checks, and privileged access management, enhancing security while improving efficiency.

Regulatory compliance remains a major driver of innovation in IGA. Governments and industry regulators continue to introduce stricter data protection and access control requirements. Organizations must ensure compliance with frameworks such as GDPR, HIPAA, SOX, and PCI DSS while maintaining operational agility. Automated compliance monitoring and reporting capabilities are becoming essential features in modern IGA platforms. Organizations are adopting real-time compliance tracking, continuous access certifications, and audit-ready reporting tools to meet regulatory requirements without manual intervention.

Another emerging trend is the increased focus on decentralized identity and self-sovereign identity (SSI). Traditional identity governance relies on centralized identity providers, which can create security risks and data privacy concerns. Decentralized identity models leverage blockchain technology to give individuals greater control over their digital identities while reducing reliance on centralized authorities. SSI solutions allow users to authenticate and access services without sharing excessive personal information, enhancing privacy and reducing identity fraud risks. While still in the early stages of adoption, decentralized identity has the potential to transform how organizations handle identity governance.

The role of behavioral analytics in identity governance is also expanding. Instead of relying solely on static access policies, organizations are implementing behavior-based identity analytics to detect unusual activity and enforce dynamic security controls. Behavioral analytics analyze login patterns, access behaviors, and transaction histories to establish a baseline of normal user activity. If a user deviates from typical behavior—such as logging in from an unfamiliar location or attempting to access restricted data—the system can trigger alerts, require additional authentication, or temporarily restrict access. This approach enhances security by proactively identifying and mitigating risks in real time.

The convergence of IGA with privileged access management (PAM) is another key trend. While traditional IGA focuses on managing standard user identities, privileged accounts require additional layers of security due to their elevated access rights. Organizations are integrating IGA and PAM solutions to enforce strict governance over privileged users, ensuring that administrative access is granted only when necessary and is continuously monitored. Implementing just-in-time (JIT) access controls, session monitoring, and automated credential rotation further reduces the risk of privilege abuse and credential-based attacks.

Identity governance is also extending to non-human identities, including service accounts, robotic process automation (RPA bots), and Internet of Things (IoT) devices. As organizations deploy more automated systems and connected devices, managing machine identities has become a critical aspect of security. IGA solutions are evolving to include governance capabilities for non-human identities, ensuring that service accounts are properly managed, permissions are regularly reviewed, and machine-to-machine communications are secured against exploitation.

Organizations are also prioritizing user experience in identity governance. Traditional identity management solutions often created friction for employees, requiring multiple logins and lengthy approval processes. Modern IGA platforms are incorporating self-service capabilities, chatbots, and AI-driven recommendations to streamline identity management. Self-service portals enable users to request access, reset passwords, and manage their profiles without IT intervention, improving efficiency while maintaining security. AI-driven decision engines assist managers in approving or denying access requests based on real-time risk assessments, reducing administrative complexity.

As cyber threats evolve, the importance of continuous monitoring and identity threat detection is becoming more apparent. Organizations are integrating identity governance with security operations centers (SOCs) and threat intelligence platforms to correlate identity-related threats with broader security incidents. Identity threat detection and response (ITDR) solutions provide real-time visibility into identity risks, enabling organizations to detect compromised credentials, mitigate insider threats, and prevent lateral movement attacks within enterprise networks.

As IGA continues to evolve, organizations must stay ahead of emerging trends to maintain security, ensure compliance, and improve operational efficiency. AI-driven identity analytics, Zero Trust frameworks, cloud-native governance, and decentralized identity models are shaping the future of identity governance. By adopting these innovations, businesses can build more resilient identity security strategies that protect their digital ecosystems while enabling seamless and secure user experiences.

Understanding the Role of Identity Analytics

Identity analytics plays a crucial role in modern identity governance and administration (IGA) by enhancing security, improving compliance, and optimizing access management. Traditional identity and access management (IAM) solutions rely on static policies and manual processes, which can be inefficient and prone to human error. Identity analytics leverages artificial intelligence (AI), machine learning (ML), and big data analysis to provide real-time insights into user behavior, detect anomalies, and automate risk-based decision-making. By integrating identity analytics into IGA frameworks, organizations can strengthen their security posture, reduce insider threats, and streamline access management processes.

One of the primary benefits of identity analytics is its ability to detect and prevent unauthorized access. Traditional access control mechanisms grant permissions based on predefined roles and policies, but they do not always account for evolving threats or unusual behavior. Identity analytics continuously monitors user activities, analyzing patterns and identifying deviations from normal access behavior. If a user suddenly accesses sensitive data outside of regular working hours or from an unusual location, identity analytics can flag the activity as suspicious and trigger additional authentication measures or access restrictions.

Risk-based authentication and access control are enhanced through identity analytics. Instead of treating all users equally, identity analytics assigns risk scores based on factors such as login patterns, device trustworthiness, geolocation, and historical behavior. High-risk users may be required to complete additional verification steps, while low-risk users can access resources with minimal friction. This adaptive security approach ensures that access decisions are dynamic and context-aware, reducing the likelihood of credential-based attacks and unauthorized access.

Identity analytics also plays a key role in insider threat detection. While external cyber threats receive significant attention, insider threats—whether intentional or accidental—pose substantial risks to organizations. Employees with excessive privileges, former employees retaining access, or compromised accounts can lead to data breaches and regulatory violations. Identity analytics identifies unusual access behaviors, such as a user downloading large volumes of data, accessing restricted systems, or frequently changing permissions. By detecting these anomalies early, organizations can take proactive measures to prevent data leaks and policy violations.

Compliance and audit readiness are strengthened through identity analytics by providing continuous visibility into user access and policy enforcement. Many regulatory frameworks, such as GDPR, HIPAA, and SOX, require organizations to maintain detailed records of access activities, conduct regular access reviews, and enforce least privilege principles. Identity analytics automates these processes by generating real-time reports, flagging non-compliant activities, and ensuring that access certifications are based on actual usage patterns rather than static role assignments. This reduces the administrative burden on compliance teams while improving overall governance.

Role mining and optimization benefit from identity analytics by ensuring that access permissions align with actual job functions. Traditional RBAC models often suffer from privilege creep, where users accumulate excessive permissions over time. Identity analytics analyzes access trends across the organization, identifying redundant roles, unused permissions, and conflicting entitlements. By refining role definitions and removing unnecessary access, organizations can improve security while maintaining operational efficiency.

User lifecycle management is another area where identity analytics enhances IGA. Organizations frequently onboard new employees, change roles, and offboard departing staff, creating potential security gaps if access is not properly managed. Identity analytics automates user provisioning and de-provisioning based on employment status, job function, and behavioral data. If an employee's role changes, access adjustments are made dynamically, reducing the risk of excessive permissions or orphaned accounts.

The integration of identity analytics with security information and event management (SIEM) solutions enhances threat detection and incident response. SIEM platforms aggregate and analyze security logs from multiple sources, including identity-related activities. Identity analytics correlates these events with user behavior data, providing a holistic view of potential security incidents. If a compromised account is detected, automated response actions—such as revoking access, triggering an incident investigation, or enforcing step-up authentication—can be initiated immediately.

Cloud adoption has increased the complexity of identity governance, requiring organizations to manage access across multiple environments. Identity analytics provides centralized visibility into cloud-based access activities, ensuring that policies are consistently enforced across SaaS applications, hybrid infrastructures, and multi-cloud platforms. By monitoring cloud-specific risks, such as excessive API calls, unauthorized data transfers, and anomalous login attempts, organizations can strengthen their security posture in cloud environments.

Artificial intelligence and machine learning continue to advance identity analytics, enabling predictive security measures and intelligent automation. ML algorithms analyze historical access patterns to predict future risks, allowing organizations to implement preemptive security controls. AI-driven automation further enhances efficiency by reducing manual intervention in access management, compliance reporting, and incident response. By continuously learning from identity-related data, these technologies help organizations adapt to evolving threats and regulatory requirements.

As identity threats become more sophisticated, identity analytics provides organizations with a data-driven approach to securing digital identities. By integrating AI-driven insights, risk-based authentication, and real-time monitoring, businesses can proactively manage user access, prevent security breaches, and ensure compliance with industry regulations. Identity analytics not only enhances security but also improves efficiency, enabling organizations to manage identities dynamically and intelligently.

Incorporating Behavioral Analysis into IGA

Identity Governance and Administration (IGA) has evolved from a static access management framework to a dynamic security approach that incorporates real-time data analysis, automation, and risk-based decision-making. As organizations face increasing cybersecurity threats, behavioral analysis has emerged as a critical component in modern IGA solutions. Traditional identity governance models rely on predefined roles and access policies, which, while effective, are often insufficient in detecting anomalies and preventing sophisticated attacks. By integrating behavioral analysis into IGA, organizations can improve threat detection, enhance access controls, and ensure continuous compliance with security policies.

Behavioral analysis in IGA leverages machine learning, artificial intelligence (AI), and analytics to monitor user activity, detect deviations from normal behavior, and assess risk levels dynamically. Instead of relying solely on static rules, this approach establishes behavioral baselines for each user based on historical access patterns, login frequency, device usage, and application interactions. When a user's activity deviates from these patterns, the system can trigger alerts, enforce additional authentication measures, or automatically adjust access privileges to mitigate potential risks.

One of the primary benefits of behavioral analysis in IGA is its ability to detect insider threats. Traditional identity governance solutions focus on external security risks, such as stolen credentials or unauthorized access attempts. However, insider threats—whether intentional or accidental—pose a significant risk to organizations. Employees with legitimate access rights can misuse privileges, escalate their permissions, or exfiltrate sensitive data without triggering traditional security alerts. By continuously monitoring behavioral patterns, IGA systems can identify anomalies such as excessive file downloads, repeated access to sensitive records, or privilege escalation attempts outside of normal work patterns.

Privileged access management (PAM) also benefits from behavioral analytics. Privileged users, such as IT administrators and executives, have elevated access rights that, if misused, can lead to significant security breaches. Traditional PAM solutions enforce strict access controls and session monitoring, but behavioral analysis adds an extra layer of protection by analyzing privileged user activity in real time. If an administrator suddenly attempts to access systems they do not typically interact with or performs actions outside of their normal schedule, the system can flag the behavior as suspicious, triggering additional authentication or temporarily suspending access until the activity is verified.

Adaptive authentication is another key application of behavioral analysis in IGA. Static authentication policies, such as requiring multi-factor authentication (MFA) for all users, can introduce unnecessary friction and impact productivity. By incorporating behavioral insights, organizations can implement risk-based authentication that adapts to user behavior. For example, if an employee accesses corporate systems from a known device and location, the system may allow seamless login without additional authentication. However, if the same user attempts to log in from an unfamiliar location or a compromised device, the system can enforce step-up authentication, such as requiring biometric verification or a one-time password (OTP). This approach improves both security and user experience by reducing authentication friction while ensuring that high-risk activities are subject to stricter controls.

Behavioral analytics also enhances compliance monitoring in IGA. Regulations such as GDPR, HIPAA, and SOX require organizations to enforce strict access controls, conduct regular audits, and ensure that user permissions align with job responsibilities. Traditional compliance audits rely on periodic reviews, which may not detect security incidents in real time. By continuously analyzing user behavior, IGA systems can provide real-time compliance insights, flagging potential violations before they escalate. If an employee accesses customer data beyond the scope of their role or an application logs an unusual volume of failed authentication attempts, the system can generate automated compliance reports and alert security teams to investigate further.

The integration of behavioral analysis with identity threat detection and response (ITDR) is another significant advancement in IGA. ITDR solutions focus on detecting and mitigating identity-based threats, including credential compromise, privilege misuse, and lateral movement attacks. By analyzing identity behaviors in real time, ITDR-powered IGA solutions can identify compromised accounts, automatically reset credentials, and enforce access restrictions before an attack progresses. Behavioral analytics also helps detect advanced persistent threats (APTs), where attackers use stolen credentials to navigate networks undetected for extended periods. By comparing user behavior against historical patterns, IGA systems can detect these subtle indicators of compromise and initiate response measures proactively.

Cloud-based IGA solutions are leveraging behavioral analysis to improve security in multi-cloud and hybrid environments. As organizations migrate to the cloud, managing identities across multiple platforms becomes increasingly complex. Traditional access governance models may struggle to enforce consistent security policies across cloud applications, on-premises systems, and third-party services. Behavioral analytics enables organizations to monitor cloud access activities in real time, detect unauthorized API requests, and enforce conditional access policies based on contextual risk factors. If a cloud-based system detects an unusually high number of failed login attempts or a spike in privileged account activity, automated response mechanisms can revoke access, notify security teams, or require additional verification.

Automated remediation is another emerging use case for behavioral analysis in IGA. Rather than relying on manual security responses, behavioral insights enable systems to take immediate action when suspicious activities are detected. For instance, if an employee's access patterns indicate potential credential compromise, the system can automatically log them out, disable their account, and force a password reset. Similarly, if a vendor's service account exhibits abnormal behavior, such as accessing data outside of business hours, the system can suspend access until an administrator verifies the legitimacy of the activity. This proactive approach minimizes security risks while reducing the burden on IT teams.

Behavioral analytics in IGA also extends to third-party risk management. Many organizations rely on contractors, partners, and suppliers who require access to internal systems. Traditional third-party access controls rely on predefined policies that may not account for evolving risks. By analyzing the behavior of third-party users, organizations can enforce dynamic access controls, restricting access when anomalous activities are detected. For example, if a vendor account suddenly accesses financial records unrelated to its role, the system can revoke access automatically and initiate an investigation. This real-time oversight enhances security while ensuring that third-party identities adhere to governance policies.

As identity-related threats continue to evolve, behavioral analysis is transforming IGA from a rule-based security model to an adaptive, intelligence-driven framework. By leveraging AI, continuous monitoring, and automated risk assessment, organizations can enhance security, streamline compliance, and reduce identity-related risks across their IT environments. The integration of behavioral insights with identity governance ensures that organizations can detect, analyze, and respond to security threats in real time, strengthening their overall cybersecurity posture.

IGA and Zero Trust Architecture

Identity Governance and Administration (IGA) plays a crucial role in the implementation of Zero Trust Architecture (ZTA), a security framework designed to eliminate implicit trust and enforce continuous verification of all users, devices, and applications. As cyber threats become more sophisticated, traditional perimeter-based security models are no longer sufficient to protect organizations from identity-related attacks, insider threats, and unauthorized access. By integrating IGA with Zero Trust principles, businesses can enhance access control, enforce least privilege policies, and ensure continuous identity verification across all environments.

Zero Trust is based on the principle of "never trust, always verify." This means that access to corporate resources is not granted based on network location or prior authentication but instead requires continuous validation of identity, security posture, and contextual factors. Traditional identity management solutions often operate on static policies and periodic access reviews, which may not be enough to prevent real-time threats. IGA enhances Zero Trust by enabling dynamic access control, risk-based authentication, and automated identity governance to ensure that users have only the permissions they need at any given time.

One of the core principles of Zero Trust is enforcing least privilege access, ensuring that users and systems are granted only the minimal permissions necessary to perform their tasks. IGA helps organizations implement least privilege by defining clear role-based access control (RBAC) and policy-based access control (PBAC) models. Automated provisioning and de-provisioning processes ensure that access rights are granted and revoked dynamically, reducing the risk of privilege creep and excessive permissions that could be exploited by malicious actors. By continuously auditing user access and enforcing time-based or conditional access policies, organizations can maintain strict control over identities in a Zero Trust environment.

Adaptive authentication and risk-based access control are essential components of Zero Trust, and IGA plays a significant role in enforcing these measures. Instead of relying solely on username and password authentication, Zero Trust incorporates multi-factor authentication (MFA), biometric verification, and behavioral analytics to assess user trustworthiness. IGA solutions integrate with authentication frameworks to analyze access requests in real time, considering factors such as device security, geolocation, time of access, and historical behavior. If an access request deviates from normal patterns, the system can require additional verification or deny access altogether, minimizing the risk of unauthorized entry.

Continuous access reviews and automated policy enforcement further strengthen Zero Trust security. Many organizations conduct periodic user access reviews to ensure that employees and contractors have appropriate permissions. However, static reviews may not be effective in detecting real-time threats or rapidly changing access requirements. IGA enables continuous monitoring of user activities, automatically flagging deviations from policy and revoking unnecessary or suspicious access. By integrating IGA with Security Information and Event Management (SIEM) systems, organizations can correlate identity-related activities with broader security events, allowing for faster detection and response to potential threats.

Privileged Access Management (PAM) is another critical aspect of Zero Trust that benefits from strong identity governance. Privileged users, such as IT administrators and executives, often have elevated access rights that make them prime targets for cyberattacks. IGA and PAM work together to enforce just-in-time (JIT) access policies, ensuring that privileged access is granted only when needed and for a limited duration. Session monitoring, credential vaulting, and automatic privilege revocation further reduce the attack surface, preventing unauthorized escalation of privileges within a Zero Trust framework.

Zero Trust is particularly relevant for organizations operating in hybrid and multi-cloud environments, where identity security must be consistently enforced across on-premises systems, SaaS applications, and cloud platforms. Cloud identity governance ensures that access controls are applied uniformly across all environments, reducing the risk of security gaps caused by misconfigured permissions. IGA solutions integrate with cloud identity providers to centralize identity management, enforce cross-platform authentication policies, and maintain visibility into cloud-based access activities.

Third-party access governance is another challenge that IGA and Zero Trust address effectively. Many organizations rely on external vendors, contractors, and service providers who require temporary or limited access to corporate resources. Traditional security models often grant excessive permissions to third parties, increasing the risk of data exposure and insider threats. By implementing Zero Trust principles, organizations can enforce strict identity verification, limit third-party access to specific applications or time frames, and continuously monitor external user activities. IGA enables automated onboarding and offboarding of third-party identities, ensuring that access is granted only when necessary and revoked as soon as it is no longer required.

Zero Trust also emphasizes continuous identity risk assessment, leveraging AI-driven identity analytics to detect anomalies and prevent unauthorized access. Identity analytics tools integrated with IGA monitor user behavior, detect unusual access patterns, and generate real-time risk scores. If a user exhibits suspicious activity, such as accessing multiple high-privilege systems in a short time or attempting to log in from an unrecognized device, the system can trigger automated security actions, such as requiring additional authentication or revoking access.

Governance and compliance remain essential in a Zero Trust framework, as organizations must adhere to regulatory requirements such as GDPR, HIPAA, and SOX. Implementing IGA within Zero Trust ensures that access policies align with compliance standards, access logs are maintained for audits, and identity-related risks are mitigated. Automated compliance reporting and access certification help organizations demonstrate adherence to security policies, reducing the risk of non-compliance penalties.

As cyber threats continue to evolve, organizations must adopt a security model that prioritizes continuous identity verification, dynamic access control, and least privilege enforcement. IGA serves as the foundation of Zero Trust, providing the necessary tools to manage user identities, enforce real-time security policies, and protect critical assets from unauthorized access. By integrating IGA with Zero Trust principles, businesses can strengthen their security posture while enabling seamless and secure access for employees, partners, and third-party users across distributed IT environments.

Building a Culture of Identity Governance

Establishing a strong culture of identity governance is essential for organizations seeking to protect sensitive information, ensure regulatory compliance, and maintain operational efficiency. Identity Governance and Administration (IGA) is not just a technical solution but a strategic approach that requires engagement across all levels of an organization. By fostering a culture that prioritizes identity governance, businesses can reduce security risks, streamline access management, and create an environment where employees, partners, and third parties understand their role in maintaining secure access to enterprise resources.

Creating a culture of identity governance begins with executive sponsorship. Leadership must recognize that identity security is not solely an IT function but a fundamental aspect of risk management and business continuity. When executives champion identity governance initiatives, they set the tone for the rest of the organization. Support from senior management helps secure the necessary investments in IGA solutions, training programs, and policy enforcement mechanisms. A top-down approach ensures that identity governance becomes a core business priority rather than an afterthought.

Employee awareness and education play a crucial role in embedding identity governance into an organization's culture. Many security breaches occur due to human error, such as weak passwords, phishing attacks, or improper handling of access credentials. Regular training sessions, awareness campaigns, and interactive workshops help employees understand the importance of secure identity management. Organizations should educate staff on best practices, such as recognizing social engineering attempts, reporting suspicious activities, and following access control policies. The more informed employees are about identity governance, the more likely they are to act responsibly when handling sensitive information.

Policy enforcement and accountability are key components of a strong identity governance culture. Organizations must establish clear policies outlining how identities are managed, who is responsible for granting and revoking access, and what actions should be taken in case of a security incident. These policies should be communicated effectively and reinforced through regular audits and compliance checks. Role-based access control (RBAC) and policy-based access control (PBAC) ensure that users only have access to the resources necessary for their job functions. Holding employees accountable for adhering to access policies fosters a sense of responsibility and reduces the likelihood of privilege misuse.

Automation and technology integration support identity governance by reducing manual workload and minimizing the risk of human error. Automated provisioning and de-provisioning of user accounts ensure that employees receive appropriate access when they join an organization and that their access is revoked promptly when they leave. Implementing multi-factor authentication (MFA), single sign-on (SSO), and adaptive authentication mechanisms further enhances security while providing a seamless user experience. AI-driven identity analytics can detect anomalies in access behavior, allowing organizations to identify potential threats before they escalate into security incidents.

Collaboration between IT, security, HR, and compliance teams is essential for maintaining a cohesive identity governance strategy. Identity governance is not an isolated function but an interdisciplinary effort that requires input from multiple departments. IT teams manage technical implementations, security teams monitor threats and enforce policies, HR teams handle employee onboarding and offboarding processes, and compliance teams ensure adherence to regulatory requirements. Regular cross-functional meetings, shared responsibility frameworks, and integrated governance workflows help organizations maintain consistency in identity management practices.

Third-party identity governance is another critical aspect of building a culture of secure access management. Many organizations rely on vendors, contractors, and business partners who require temporary access to enterprise systems. Without proper oversight, third-party identities can become a security risk, particularly if access permissions are not revoked after a contract ends. Establishing strict policies for third-party access, enforcing least privilege principles, and continuously monitoring external user activity help organizations mitigate risks associated with supply chain security.

Metrics and continuous improvement drive long-term success in identity governance. Organizations should define key performance indicators (KPIs) to measure the effectiveness of their IGA programs. Metrics such as the time required to revoke access for departing employees, the completion rate of access reviews, and the number of policy violations detected provide insights into areas that need improvement. Regular assessments and audits help refine identity governance policies, ensuring they remain aligned with evolving business needs and regulatory changes.

Leadership commitment, employee engagement, policy enforcement, automation, cross-functional collaboration, and continuous improvement are all essential elements of a strong identity governance culture. When organizations prioritize identity governance at every level, they create a security-conscious workforce, reduce risks associated with unauthorized access, and ensure that identity management practices align with business objectives. By integrating identity governance into the corporate culture, organizations establish a foundation for secure and efficient digital operations.

Overcoming Resistance to IGA Initiatives

Implementing Identity Governance and Administration (IGA) is a critical step in securing enterprise systems, enforcing compliance, and streamlining identity management. However, organizations often face resistance when introducing IGA initiatives. This resistance may stem from employees, IT teams, or leadership, each of whom may have concerns about usability, disruption, or cost. Overcoming these challenges requires a structured approach that focuses on communication, education, strategic implementation, and continuous engagement with stakeholders.

One of the most common sources of resistance comes from employees who fear that IGA initiatives will complicate their daily workflows. When new security controls, access restrictions, or authentication measures are introduced, employees may perceive them as unnecessary obstacles rather than security enhancements. Organizations can address these concerns by providing clear explanations of why identity governance is necessary, how it protects both individual and company data, and what steps have been taken to minimize disruptions. Conducting awareness campaigns, offering training sessions, and demonstrating the benefits of streamlined access request processes can help employees view IGA as a positive change rather than a burden.

IT teams may also resist IGA initiatives, particularly if they believe the implementation will introduce operational complexity, require extensive configuration, or demand additional resources. Many IT professionals are accustomed to legacy systems and manual access management processes, and transitioning to an automated IGA platform can seem daunting. To gain IT support, organizations should involve IT teams early in the selection and planning phases, ensuring that they have a voice in decision-making. Providing hands-on training, outlining the efficiencies gained through automation, and highlighting the reduction in manual administrative tasks can help IT professionals see the value in adopting IGA.

Leadership and executive teams may hesitate to approve IGA initiatives due to concerns about cost, return on investment (ROI), and business impact. Decision-makers often prioritize initiatives that drive revenue and growth, and identity governance may not always be viewed as an immediate business enabler. Demonstrating the financial and operational benefits of IGA is key to securing executive buy-in. This includes emphasizing cost savings from reduced administrative workload, mitigating financial risks associated with security breaches, and improving compliance to avoid regulatory penalties. Presenting case studies of successful IGA deployments in similar industries can further support the business case.

Another significant challenge in IGA adoption is resistance to change. Employees and teams that have relied on traditional access management methods for years may be reluctant to transition to a new system. Change management strategies play a crucial role in addressing this resistance. Organizations should implement IGA initiatives gradually, allowing time for adaptation. A phased rollout approach, where identity governance is introduced in manageable stages, can ease the transition. Starting with high-risk areas such as privileged access management before expanding to broader user groups can demonstrate the effectiveness of IGA while minimizing resistance.

Communication is essential in overcoming resistance to IGA initiatives. Organizations should ensure that messaging about the project is clear, consistent, and tailored to different audiences. Technical teams may require detailed explanations of how the system integrates with existing infrastructure, while business users may need a simplified overview of how it improves efficiency. Regular updates through emails, town halls, and training sessions keep stakeholders informed and engaged throughout the implementation process.

User experience is another factor that influences resistance to IGA adoption. If the system is difficult to navigate or adds unnecessary complexity to everyday tasks, users may be less willing to embrace it. Organizations should prioritize user-friendly interfaces, self-service access management tools, and streamlined approval workflows. Conducting usability testing before deployment helps identify pain points and refine the system based on user feedback. Ensuring that access requests, password resets, and role assignments are intuitive and efficient enhances user adoption.

Security fatigue can contribute to resistance, particularly in organizations where employees are already overwhelmed with authentication requirements, password policies, and compliance procedures. Introducing IGA as a way to simplify security rather than add to the burden can shift perceptions. Features such as single sign-on (SSO), automated access provisioning, and contextual authentication can reduce friction while maintaining strong security controls. Organizations should highlight these benefits to demonstrate how IGA enhances user experience rather than complicating it.

Engaging internal champions can help drive IGA adoption. Identifying influential employees, IT leaders, or department heads who understand the value of identity governance can accelerate acceptance within teams. These champions can act as advocates, helping to communicate benefits, address concerns, and encourage others to adopt new identity governance practices. When employees see peers embracing IGA, they are more likely to follow suit.

Providing measurable success indicators reinforces the value of IGA initiatives. Organizations should track and communicate key metrics, such as reduced security incidents, faster access approvals, and improved compliance scores. Demonstrating quick wins, such as automating user onboarding processes or reducing audit findings, helps build confidence in the initiative. Transparency in reporting progress fosters trust and reassures stakeholders that the implementation is delivering tangible benefits.

Aligning IGA with broader business objectives further strengthens its adoption. When identity governance is positioned as a key enabler of digital transformation, cloud security, and regulatory compliance, stakeholders recognize its strategic importance. Integrating IGA with existing security frameworks, such as Zero Trust or risk-based authentication, reinforces its role in protecting enterprise assets while supporting business growth.

Long-term sustainability of IGA initiatives requires continuous improvement. Organizations should regularly solicit user feedback, refine policies, and adapt governance frameworks to evolving security threats and business needs. Establishing a governance committee or working group dedicated to IGA ensures that identity governance remains a priority beyond the initial implementation phase.

By addressing concerns proactively, engaging stakeholders at all levels, and demonstrating clear value, organizations can successfully overcome resistance to IGA initiatives. A thoughtful, user-centric approach ensures that identity governance becomes an integral part of business operations, fostering a culture of security, efficiency, and compliance.

Measuring the ROI of IGA

Implementing an Identity Governance and Administration (IGA) solution is a strategic investment for organizations aiming to strengthen security, improve compliance, and streamline identity management processes. While the benefits of IGA are widely recognized, measuring its return on investment (ROI) is essential to justify costs, demonstrate value to stakeholders, and optimize ongoing efforts. Calculating the ROI of IGA requires evaluating both direct and indirect benefits, considering cost savings, risk reduction, operational efficiency, and compliance improvements.

One of the most significant factors in IGA's ROI is cost reduction through automation. Traditional identity management processes rely heavily on manual interventions, requiring IT administrators to handle user provisioning, de-provisioning, access requests, and compliance audits manually. These tasks consume valuable resources and increase the likelihood of errors. By automating identity lifecycle management, organizations reduce administrative overhead, lower labor costs, and minimize the need for costly corrections due to access mismanagement. The time savings achieved by automation translate directly into financial savings, improving the overall efficiency of IT operations.

Improved security posture is another key component of IGA's ROI. Identity-related breaches, such as credential theft, insider threats, and privilege misuse, are among the most costly security incidents organizations face. Unauthorized access to sensitive systems can lead to financial loss, reputational damage, and regulatory penalties. By enforcing least privilege access, automating access reviews, and continuously monitoring user activities, IGA reduces the likelihood of breaches and associated remediation costs. Quantifying the ROI of improved security involves assessing the potential financial impact of breaches that have been prevented due to strong identity governance practices.

IGA also enhances regulatory compliance, reducing the risk of fines and penalties associated with non-compliance. Many industries are subject to strict regulations such as GDPR, HIPAA, SOX, and PCI DSS, which require organizations to enforce access controls, conduct regular audits, and maintain detailed records of identity-related activities. Manual compliance processes are resource-intensive and prone to errors, increasing the risk of regulatory violations. IGA solutions automate compliance reporting, streamline audit preparation, and ensure continuous enforcement of access policies. Measuring ROI in this area involves comparing the costs of compliance-related efforts before and after IGA implementation, as well as calculating potential savings from avoiding regulatory penalties.

Operational efficiency gains contribute significantly to the financial benefits of IGA. Employees, contractors, and third-party users need timely access to enterprise systems to perform their tasks effectively. Delays in provisioning access or resolving access issues can lead to lost productivity, frustration, and inefficiencies across departments. Self-service access management, automated role assignments, and real-time access monitoring enable organizations to accelerate onboarding, facilitate seamless role changes, and prevent unnecessary downtime. The resulting productivity improvements can be quantified by evaluating the reduction in time spent on access management tasks and the increase in workforce efficiency.

Privileged access management (PAM) integration further enhances the financial benefits of IGA. Privileged accounts are high-risk targets for cyberattacks, and improper management of these accounts can lead to significant security incidents. IGA solutions that incorporate PAM ensure that privileged access is granted only when necessary, with strict monitoring and session recording to prevent misuse. By reducing the risk of privileged account compromise, organizations avoid potential financial losses associated with unauthorized administrative access, system disruptions, and data breaches.

Identity analytics and risk-based decision-making add another dimension to IGA's ROI. Traditional access controls often grant permissions based on static policies, which may not always account for evolving security threats. AI-driven identity analytics enhance decision-making by continuously assessing user behavior, flagging anomalies, and adjusting access rights based on real-time risk assessments. This proactive approach reduces the need for manual security interventions, minimizes false positives in access requests, and improves overall security without adding operational complexity. Measuring ROI in this area involves analyzing reductions in security incidents, the speed of threat detection, and the efficiency of automated responses.

Third-party access governance is an additional area where IGA delivers measurable financial benefits. Many organizations work with external vendors, contractors, and partners who require temporary access to enterprise systems. Without proper governance, third-party accounts can remain active longer than needed, increasing the risk of security incidents. IGA automates third-party identity lifecycle management, ensuring that access is granted based on business needs and revoked when no longer required. Organizations can measure ROI by assessing reductions in unauthorized third-party access, improvements in vendor compliance, and efficiency gains in managing external identities.

Cloud security and hybrid environment management further contribute to the ROI of IGA. As organizations transition to cloud-based services, managing identities across multiple environments becomes increasingly complex. IGA solutions that support cloud identity management ensure consistent access controls across on-premises, SaaS, and multi-cloud platforms. By centralizing identity governance, organizations reduce the risk of cloud security misconfigurations, improve policy enforcement, and enhance visibility into user access patterns. The financial benefits of cloud-integrated IGA can be measured by analyzing reductions in cloud security incidents, faster response times to access anomalies, and improved overall governance of digital identities.

User experience improvements provide additional indirect financial benefits. Frictionless access to applications and data enhances employee satisfaction, reducing frustration related to password resets, access delays, and compliance-related disruptions. Self-service portals, single sign-on (SSO), and adaptive authentication reduce helpdesk requests and minimize productivity losses due to access-related issues. Organizations can measure ROI by calculating reductions in IT support tickets, improvements in employee satisfaction scores, and the overall impact on operational efficiency.

Quantifying the ROI of IGA requires a combination of direct cost savings, risk reduction metrics, and operational efficiency improvements. Organizations can track key performance indicators (KPIs) such as the time required for user onboarding, the number of security incidents prevented, the cost savings from compliance automation, and the reduction in administrative workload for IT teams. By continuously evaluating these metrics, businesses can demonstrate the value of IGA and make informed decisions about optimizing identity governance strategies for long-term success.

Future Directions in IGA

Identity Governance and Administration (IGA) is evolving rapidly as organizations navigate increasing cybersecurity threats, regulatory requirements, and digital transformation initiatives. The future of IGA is shaped by advancements in artificial intelligence, automation, decentralized identity models, and the growing adoption of Zero Trust frameworks. As the complexity of IT environments continues to expand, businesses must adapt their identity governance strategies to ensure security, compliance, and operational efficiency. Emerging trends in IGA will redefine how organizations manage identities, enforce access controls, and respond to security risks.

Artificial intelligence and machine learning are playing a central role in the evolution of IGA. Traditional identity governance relies on static access policies and manual reviews, which can be time-consuming and prone to human error. AI-driven identity analytics enhance IGA by continuously monitoring user behavior, detecting anomalies, and providing risk-based access recommendations. Machine learning algorithms help organizations automate access reviews, predict potential security threats, and optimize role-based access control (RBAC) models. By leveraging AI for identity governance, businesses can reduce administrative overhead, improve security posture, and respond more effectively to evolving cyber threats.

The integration of IGA with Zero Trust security architectures is becoming a priority for organizations looking to strengthen identity protection. Zero Trust operates on the principle of continuous verification, ensuring that no user or device is implicitly trusted. Future IGA solutions will incorporate dynamic risk assessments, adaptive authentication mechanisms, and real-time policy enforcement to align with Zero Trust principles. Organizations will need to implement continuous identity verification processes that go beyond static credentials, incorporating factors such as behavioral analytics, device security posture, and contextual access control. This approach will help mitigate risks associated with credential theft, insider threats, and unauthorized access attempts.

Decentralized identity and self-sovereign identity (SSI) are emerging as transformative concepts in identity governance. Traditional identity management relies on centralized directories and identity providers, which can introduce security risks and privacy concerns. Decentralized identity solutions leverage blockchain technology and cryptographic credentials to enable users to control their digital identities without relying on a single authority. This shift will empower individuals to authenticate securely across multiple platforms while reducing the risk of identity theft and data breaches. As decentralized identity standards mature, organizations will need to integrate SSI models into their IGA frameworks to support privacy-enhancing authentication methods.

Cloud-native IGA is becoming essential as businesses continue to migrate to cloud environments. Legacy identity governance solutions designed for on-premises infrastructure struggle to manage the complexity of hybrid and multi-cloud ecosystems. Future IGA platforms will be designed with cloud-native architectures, offering scalability, automation, and integration with identity-as-a-service (IDaaS) providers. These solutions will provide centralized visibility and policy enforcement across on-premises, cloud, and SaaS applications, ensuring that identity governance remains consistent in distributed IT environments.

The rise of non-human identities, including service accounts, robotic process automation (RPA), and Internet of Things (IoT) devices, is changing the landscape of identity governance. Traditional IGA frameworks have focused primarily on human users, but the increasing use of automated systems and connected devices requires a shift in governance strategies. Future IGA solutions will incorporate machine identity management, ensuring that service accounts and bots are governed with the same level of security and oversight as human identities. Organizations will need to implement automated lifecycle management for non-human identities, enforce least privilege access, and monitor machine-to-machine interactions for suspicious behavior.

Identity threat detection and response (ITDR) is emerging as a critical component of future IGA strategies. Cybercriminals are increasingly targeting identity-based attack vectors, such as phishing, credential stuffing, and privilege escalation. ITDR integrates identity governance with advanced threat detection capabilities, enabling organizations to identify compromised accounts, detect lateral movement, and respond to identity-related security incidents in real time. Future IGA platforms will incorporate AI-driven threat intelligence, anomaly detection, and automated response mechanisms to enhance identity security and mitigate attack risks before they escalate.

Regulatory compliance will continue to shape the future of IGA, with stricter data protection laws and industry regulations driving the need for more sophisticated identity governance solutions. Organizations must comply with evolving frameworks such as GDPR, CCPA, HIPAA, and NIST standards, requiring continuous monitoring, audit readiness, and policy enforcement. Future IGA platforms will offer automated compliance tracking, real-time risk assessments, and audit reporting tools to help businesses maintain regulatory adherence while minimizing manual effort. The integration of compliance automation with IGA will streamline governance processes and reduce the complexity of regulatory audits.

User experience and identity self-service capabilities will become increasingly important in the next generation of IGA solutions. Employees, contractors, and third-party partners expect seamless access to applications and services without unnecessary friction. Future IGA platforms will incorporate AI-powered chatbots, self-service portals, and personalized access recommendations to improve user experience while maintaining security. Adaptive access management will ensure that users receive appropriate permissions based on real-time risk analysis, reducing the need for manual intervention while preventing unauthorized access.

As the digital workforce expands and remote work becomes the norm, organizations will need to adopt more flexible identity governance strategies. Future IGA solutions will support workforce mobility by enabling secure access from any location, device, or network. Conditional access policies, geofencing, and risk-based authentication will play a crucial role in ensuring that employees can work securely while maintaining compliance with organizational security policies. The ability to dynamically adjust access privileges based on user context will enhance both security and productivity in distributed work environments.

The convergence of IGA with identity lifecycle automation will further streamline identity governance processes. Automating user onboarding, access requests, and role adjustments will reduce the administrative burden on IT and security teams while ensuring that access policies remain aligned with business requirements. Future IGA platforms will leverage AI-driven workflows, intelligent role mining, and policy-based automation to enable organizations to manage identities at scale without compromising security. The shift toward autonomous identity governance will allow businesses to proactively manage access risks and enforce security controls with minimal manual oversight.

The future of IGA is centered on automation, intelligence, and adaptability. As organizations face increasingly complex identity governance challenges, the integration of AI, Zero Trust, decentralized identity, and cloud-native architectures will drive the next generation of identity governance solutions. Businesses that embrace these innovations will enhance security, improve compliance, and create a more efficient identity management ecosystem capable of adapting to emerging threats and evolving regulatory landscapes.

Scaling IGA for Global Enterprises

As organizations expand globally, the complexity of managing identities, access controls, and compliance requirements increases significantly. Identity Governance and Administration (IGA) plays a crucial role in ensuring that enterprises can manage user identities efficiently across multiple regions, regulatory environments, and IT ecosystems. Scaling IGA for global enterprises requires a strategy that balances security, efficiency, and regulatory adherence while addressing the unique challenges associated with large-scale identity management.

One of the primary challenges in scaling IGA for global enterprises is managing a diverse and distributed workforce. Employees, contractors, and third-party vendors operate across different time zones, languages, and regulatory jurisdictions, making identity governance more complex. Organizations must implement a centralized IGA framework that provides consistency while allowing for regional flexibility. This means defining global identity policies while enabling local adjustments to meet country-specific regulations and operational needs. By leveraging a federated identity management approach, enterprises can maintain uniform governance standards without imposing rigid policies that hinder business operations.

Regulatory compliance adds another layer of complexity to scaling IGA globally. Different regions have varying data protection laws, such as the General Data Protection Regulation (GDPR) in Europe, the California Consumer Privacy Act (CCPA) in the United States, and China's Personal Information Protection Law (PIPL). A scalable IGA solution must enforce compliance with multiple regulatory frameworks while ensuring that identity governance policies align with corporate security standards. This requires automated compliance tracking, real-time access reviews, and localized reporting capabilities to support audits in different jurisdictions.

The shift to hybrid and multi-cloud environments further complicates identity governance at a global scale. Enterprises utilize a combination of on-premises infrastructure, cloud services, and third-party SaaS applications, each with different identity management requirements. A scalable IGA strategy must integrate with multiple identity providers, cloud platforms, and on-premises directories to provide a seamless identity governance experience. Implementing identity federation, single sign-on (SSO), and centralized access control policies ensures that users can securely access resources across various environments without creating security gaps.

Automation is a key enabler of scalable IGA, reducing the administrative burden associated with managing identities across a global workforce. Automated provisioning and de-provisioning ensure that users receive appropriate access based on their role, department, and location. By integrating artificial intelligence (AI) and machine learning (ML), enterprises can enhance identity governance through intelligent role mining, anomaly detection, and risk-based access control. AI-driven IGA solutions analyze user behavior to identify excessive permissions, detect unusual access requests, and recommend policy adjustments in real time.

A risk-based approach to identity governance enhances scalability by prioritizing security efforts based on real-time identity risk assessments. Instead of applying uniform access policies across all users, enterprises can implement dynamic access controls that adjust permissions based on contextual factors such as user location, device security, and authentication history. Risk-based authentication and adaptive access management ensure that high-risk access requests undergo additional verification steps, reducing the likelihood of unauthorized access while minimizing friction for low-risk users.

Managing privileged access at a global scale requires additional governance controls. IT administrators, executives, and other high-privilege users often require access to critical systems across multiple regions. Without proper oversight, privileged accounts can become major security risks, particularly in large organizations with decentralized IT operations. Implementing Privileged Access Management (PAM) alongside IGA helps enforce strict access policies, monitor privileged sessions, and ensure that high-risk activities are logged and reviewed. Just-in-time (JIT) access provisioning further strengthens security by granting temporary access only when needed and revoking it automatically after use.

Ensuring a positive user experience is essential when scaling IGA for global enterprises. While strong identity governance is necessary for security, it should not create unnecessary barriers to productivity. Implementing self-service identity management capabilities, such as password resets, access requests, and identity verification, empowers users to manage their own identities without relying on IT support. A well-designed IGA solution should provide localized user interfaces, multilingual support, and region-specific workflows to accommodate a diverse global workforce.

Identity governance also extends to external partners, suppliers, and customers who require access to enterprise systems. Third-party access governance becomes increasingly complex at a global scale, as organizations must manage identities that fall outside traditional corporate structures. Implementing third-party identity lifecycle management ensures that external users receive appropriate access while enforcing strict authentication and monitoring controls. Automated onboarding and offboarding processes help reduce security risks by ensuring that third-party access is revoked immediately when no longer needed.

Real-time monitoring and analytics play a crucial role in scaling IGA by providing continuous visibility into identity-related risks and activities. Security Information and Event Management (SIEM) systems, combined with identity threat detection and response (ITDR) capabilities, allow enterprises to detect and mitigate identity-based threats before they escalate. Continuous monitoring of access patterns, failed authentication attempts, and privilege escalations enables security teams to respond proactively to potential breaches.

IGA must also support mergers, acquisitions, and organizational restructuring, which are common in large global enterprises. When companies merge or acquire new entities, integrating disparate identity systems can be a major challenge. A scalable IGA framework ensures seamless identity consolidation by mapping existing access rights, eliminating redundant accounts, and enforcing unified security policies across the newly integrated organization. This prevents security gaps and ensures compliance with corporate governance standards.

To future-proof identity governance, enterprises must adopt a flexible and scalable IGA architecture that can adapt to evolving business needs, regulatory changes, and emerging security threats. Cloud-native IGA solutions provide the agility required to scale identity governance dynamically while reducing infrastructure overhead. By continuously improving identity governance strategies, enterprises can strengthen security, ensure regulatory compliance, and support global business operations efficiently.

Maintaining Security While Driving Innovation

Organizations today face the dual challenge of fostering innovation while ensuring robust security measures. As businesses embrace digital transformation, cloud computing, artificial intelligence, and automation, maintaining security without hindering progress becomes a delicate balancing act. Traditional security models often emphasize rigid controls that can slow down innovation, while unregulated experimentation can lead to increased vulnerabilities. A well-designed identity governance and administration (IGA) strategy helps organizations integrate security seamlessly into their innovation processes, ensuring that new technologies and business initiatives do not introduce unnecessary risks.

One of the primary ways organizations can maintain security while driving innovation is by embedding security into the development lifecycle. DevOps teams must adopt a security-first mindset, implementing security measures from the earliest stages of software and product development. Secure DevOps, or DevSecOps, integrates security controls into continuous integration and continuous deployment (CI/CD) pipelines, ensuring that vulnerabilities are identified and mitigated before new applications or features go live. Automated security testing, identity access controls, and policy enforcement reduce the likelihood of security gaps while maintaining development speed.

Identity governance plays a crucial role in securing innovation-driven environments by enforcing role-based access control (RBAC) and policy-based access control (PBAC). Employees working on cutting-edge projects often require access to sensitive systems, experimental platforms, and proprietary data. Without proper governance, excessive or unchecked access can create security blind spots. Implementing dynamic access controls ensures that employees, contractors, and partners receive the right level of access based on their roles, responsibilities, and risk profiles. Context-aware access policies help organizations maintain security without limiting collaboration and innovation.

Cloud adoption is a major driver of innovation, allowing businesses to scale operations, improve efficiency, and experiment with new technologies. However, managing security in cloud environments presents unique challenges, particularly regarding identity and access management. Traditional perimeter-based security models are ineffective in hybrid and multi-cloud architectures, where users, applications, and workloads operate across different platforms. Implementing cloud-native IGA solutions ensures that security policies remain consistent across all cloud environments. Single sign-on (SSO), multi-factor authentication (MFA), and federated identity management provide seamless yet secure access to cloud-based resources.

Artificial intelligence and machine learning are transforming industries, enabling automation, predictive analytics, and enhanced decision-making. However, AI-driven innovations require access to vast amounts of data, increasing the need for stringent security controls. Organizations must ensure that AI models do not inadvertently expose sensitive data or violate compliance requirements. Identity analytics enhances security by monitoring AI system access, detecting anomalies, and enforcing data protection policies. By integrating AI-driven security monitoring with IGA, organizations can leverage the benefits of AI while maintaining control over data access and identity-related risks.

Innovation often involves collaboration with external partners, vendors, and research institutions. While these partnerships accelerate technological advancements, they also introduce third-party security risks. Managing external identities securely is critical to preventing unauthorized access and data breaches. Implementing third-party access governance ensures that vendors and partners are granted limited access based on business needs and contractual agreements. Automated provisioning and de-provisioning workflows help enforce temporary access policies, ensuring that third parties do not retain access beyond the duration of their engagement.

Security awareness and cultural transformation are equally important in balancing security with innovation. Employees, developers, and business leaders must understand that security is not an obstacle to progress but an enabler of sustainable growth. Organizations should promote a culture where security best practices are ingrained into daily operations. Regular training, awareness programs, and security champions within innovation teams can reinforce secure behaviors. Encouraging secure coding practices, conducting phishing simulations, and implementing just-in-time (JIT) security training ensures that employees remain vigilant against emerging threats.

Zero Trust security models align well with innovation-driven organizations by enforcing continuous authentication, least privilege access, and micro-segmentation. Unlike traditional security models that assume trust within network perimeters, Zero Trust verifies every access request based on user behavior, device security posture, and contextual risk factors. Implementing Zero Trust in identity governance ensures that only authorized users can interact with critical systems, reducing the risk of insider threats and lateral movement attacks. By integrating Zero Trust principles into innovation strategies, organizations can enable agility while maintaining strong security controls.

Regulatory compliance remains a challenge for organizations pursuing innovation in highly regulated industries such as healthcare, finance, and government. Compliance requirements often dictate strict access controls, audit trails, and data protection measures that may seem restrictive to innovation teams. However, modern IGA solutions simplify compliance by automating access certifications, enforcing policy-based access, and providing real-time audit reports. By embedding compliance into security frameworks, organizations can ensure that innovation efforts align with regulatory expectations without compromising agility.

Incident response and risk mitigation strategies must evolve alongside innovation efforts. As new technologies introduce unforeseen vulnerabilities, organizations must be prepared to detect and respond to security incidents in real time. Identity threat detection and response (ITDR) solutions provide visibility into identity-related threats, enabling organizations to detect compromised credentials, privilege escalation attempts, and unauthorized access patterns. By integrating IGA with ITDR capabilities, businesses can minimize the impact of security incidents while maintaining operational resilience.

Organizations that successfully balance security with innovation recognize that both objectives are interconnected rather than conflicting. When security is seamlessly integrated into development, cloud adoption, AI-driven processes, and third-party collaborations, innovation can thrive without exposing the business to unnecessary risks. Investing in identity governance, adopting Zero Trust principles, and fostering a culture of security awareness ensure that organizations can drive technological advancements while safeguarding their digital ecosystems.

Building a Resilient Identity Governance Ecosystem

A resilient identity governance ecosystem is essential for organizations seeking to secure digital assets, enforce compliance, and support operational efficiency. As cyber threats evolve, regulatory requirements become stricter, and IT environments grow more complex, businesses must develop identity governance frameworks that can withstand disruptions, adapt to change, and ensure seamless access management. By integrating automation, intelligence, and proactive risk management into identity governance and administration (IGA), organizations can build a system that remains effective under pressure while aligning with business objectives.

Resilience in identity governance begins with a well-defined strategy that accounts for scalability, flexibility, and risk mitigation. Organizations must establish clear policies that define how identities are managed throughout their lifecycle, from provisioning and access requests to role changes and de-provisioning. A structured approach ensures that identity governance practices are applied consistently across all users, including employees, contractors, third-party vendors, and non-human identities such as service accounts and robotic process automation (RPA) bots. A resilient ecosystem requires continuous evaluation and refinement of these policies to accommodate new security threats, regulatory changes, and business transformations.

Automation is a critical component of a resilient IGA ecosystem. Manual identity management processes are not only inefficient but also prone to human error, increasing security risks and compliance gaps. Automated workflows for user provisioning, role assignments, and access reviews streamline identity governance while reducing administrative overhead. Intelligent automation, powered by artificial intelligence and machine learning, enhances identity governance by detecting anomalous behavior, recommending policy adjustments, and dynamically enforcing security controls. Organizations that leverage automation effectively can respond more quickly to security threats and maintain continuous compliance with minimal manual intervention.

Risk-based access control strengthens the adaptability of an identity governance framework by dynamically adjusting access permissions based on real-time risk assessments. Traditional static role-based access control (RBAC) models may not provide sufficient agility in rapidly changing IT environments. By incorporating policy-based access control (PBAC) and AI-driven risk scoring, organizations can grant or restrict access based on contextual factors such as device security posture, user location, and behavioral analytics. This approach ensures that identity governance remains proactive rather than reactive, allowing organizations to mitigate risks before they escalate into security incidents.

Integration with Zero Trust architecture enhances the resilience of identity governance by eliminating implicit trust and enforcing continuous verification of users, devices, and applications. A Zero Trust model ensures that access to enterprise resources is based on identity verification, contextual risk assessments, and strict access policies. By aligning IGA with Zero Trust principles, organizations can enforce least privilege access, require multi-factor authentication (MFA) for high-risk activities, and continuously monitor user activity to detect suspicious behavior. A resilient identity governance ecosystem incorporates Zero Trust as a foundational principle, ensuring that security remains dynamic and adaptive.

Cloud adoption and hybrid IT environments introduce new challenges for identity governance, requiring organizations to establish a unified approach to managing identities across multiple platforms. A resilient

IGA strategy extends governance beyond on-premises systems to include cloud applications, SaaS platforms, and multi-cloud infrastructures. Cloud-native identity governance solutions provide centralized visibility and policy enforcement across all environments, reducing security gaps caused by fragmented identity management practices. Federated identity management and single sign-on (SSO) further enhance resilience by simplifying authentication processes while maintaining strong security controls.

Third-party and vendor identity governance must also be integrated into a resilient ecosystem. Many organizations rely on external partners, contractors, and suppliers who require access to critical business applications. Without proper governance, third-party access can become a major security risk, especially if permissions are not revoked after contracts expire. A robust IGA framework includes automated workflows for onboarding and offboarding third-party users, enforcing least privilege access, and continuously monitoring external identities for suspicious activities. Establishing clear policies for third-party risk management ensures that external access remains controlled and aligned with security best practices.

Identity threat detection and response (ITDR) enhances resilience by providing real-time visibility into identity-based risks and enabling organizations to respond quickly to potential threats. ITDR solutions integrate with IGA to detect compromised accounts, unusual access patterns, and privilege misuse. By correlating identity-related security events with broader cybersecurity intelligence, organizations can identify threats earlier and take immediate action to prevent data breaches. Automated incident response mechanisms, such as revoking compromised credentials or enforcing additional authentication requirements, further strengthen an organization's ability to mitigate identity-related risks.

Compliance automation plays a vital role in maintaining a resilient identity governance framework. Regulatory requirements continue to evolve, placing greater emphasis on access control, data protection, and auditability. A modern IGA ecosystem automates compliance reporting, access certifications, and audit trails, reducing the burden on security and compliance teams. By leveraging AI-driven analytics, organizations can identify potential compliance violations before they result in penalties, ensuring continuous adherence to industry standards such as GDPR, HIPAA, and SOX.

User experience is a crucial consideration in designing a resilient IGA framework. While security and compliance are top priorities, organizations must ensure that identity governance does not create unnecessary friction for employees, customers, or partners. Self-service portals, passwordless authentication options, and context-aware access controls improve the user experience while maintaining security. Adaptive authentication mechanisms allow users to access resources seamlessly under normal conditions while enforcing stricter security measures when risk levels increase. A user-centric approach to identity governance encourages compliance with security policies while promoting efficiency.

Organizations must also future-proof their identity governance ecosystems by embracing emerging technologies and evolving security best practices. As identity threats become more sophisticated, IGA frameworks must be capable of integrating with advanced security solutions such as behavioral analytics, AI-driven anomaly detection, and blockchain-based decentralized identity models. Regularly assessing and updating identity governance policies, investing in workforce training, and fostering a security-conscious culture further contribute to building a sustainable and resilient identity governance ecosystem.

By prioritizing automation, risk-based access control, Zero Trust integration, cloud security, third-party governance, ITDR, compliance automation, and user experience, organizations can establish an identity governance framework that adapts to evolving threats and operational demands. A resilient identity governance ecosystem is not just a security measure—it is a strategic advantage that ensures the organization remains agile, compliant, and protected in an increasingly complex digital landscape.

IGA as a Continuous Process

Identity Governance and Administration (IGA) is not a one-time initiative but an ongoing process that requires continuous refinement, monitoring, and adaptation. Organizations operate in dynamic environments where workforce changes, evolving cybersecurity threats, regulatory updates, and technological advancements constantly impact identity governance requirements. Treating IGA as a continuous process ensures that organizations maintain compliance, reduce security risks, and optimize access management without introducing unnecessary friction to business operations.

A key reason for adopting a continuous approach to IGA is the ever-changing nature of user identities and access needs. Employees join, leave, or change roles within an organization, requiring immediate updates to their access privileges. Contractors and third-party vendors also require temporary access, which must be carefully managed and revoked once their engagement ends. Without continuous oversight, organizations risk privilege creep, orphaned accounts, and unauthorized access to sensitive systems. Automating identity lifecycle management ensures that access rights are provisioned and de-provisioned dynamically, reducing human error and improving overall security.

Regulatory compliance is another driving factor behind the need for ongoing identity governance. Data protection laws such as GDPR, HIPAA, and SOX require organizations to maintain strict access controls, conduct regular audits, and ensure accountability for identity-related actions. A static approach to IGA may leave organizations vulnerable to compliance violations if policies are not updated to reflect changing regulations. Continuous monitoring and automated compliance reporting allow businesses to track access patterns, detect anomalies, and generate audit-ready documentation in real time. By integrating identity governance with compliance automation tools, organizations can adapt to new regulatory requirements without disrupting operations.

Security threats targeting digital identities continue to evolve, making it essential to treat IGA as a continuous security function. Cybercriminals frequently exploit weak identity controls through credential theft, phishing attacks, and insider threats. Organizations must implement continuous access reviews, real-time identity threat detection, and automated remediation mechanisms to mitigate these risks. AI-driven identity analytics play a crucial role in identifying suspicious behavior, such as unusual login locations, excessive permission requests, or unauthorized privilege escalations. By analyzing identity-related risks continuously, organizations can take proactive measures to prevent security incidents before they escalate.

IGA also plays a crucial role in enforcing least privilege access and Zero Trust security principles. Traditional access control models often grant broad permissions based on static role definitions, which can lead to excessive access accumulation over time. A continuous approach to IGA incorporates risk-based access control (RBAC and PBAC), adaptive authentication, and just-in-time (JIT) access provisioning to ensure that users receive only the permissions necessary for their specific tasks. Regular access reviews and policy adjustments prevent over-privileged accounts from becoming security liabilities.

Cloud adoption and hybrid IT environments further emphasize the need for ongoing identity governance. As organizations migrate workloads to cloud platforms, managing identities across multiple environments becomes increasingly complex. Cloud-native IGA solutions provide real-time visibility into access activities, enforce consistent security policies across on-premises and cloud applications, and integrate with identity providers such as Azure AD, Okta, and AWS IAM. Continuous synchronization of identity data ensures that users have seamless and secure access to resources without exposing the organization to security gaps.

The integration of IGA with Security Information and Event Management (SIEM) and Identity Threat Detection and Response (ITDR) platforms strengthens security by correlating identity-related events with broader cybersecurity incidents. Continuous identity governance allows security teams to detect patterns of malicious activity, such as credential stuffing attacks, privilege misuse, and insider threats. Automating responses—such as revoking compromised credentials, enforcing step-up authentication, or blocking suspicious access attempts—reduces the impact of security breaches and improves overall resilience.

User experience remains an important consideration in continuous identity governance. Employees and business users expect seamless access to applications and services without unnecessary delays or security roadblocks. Implementing self-service access request portals, passwordless authentication, and AI-driven access recommendations enhances usability while maintaining strong governance controls. A continuous approach to IGA ensures that security and user convenience remain balanced, enabling organizations to support digital transformation initiatives without compromising identity security.

Continuous identity governance also extends to non-human identities, such as service accounts, robotic process automation (RPA) bots, and IoT devices. These identities require strict governance to prevent unauthorized access and credential misuse. Implementing automated lifecycle management, periodic access recertification, and continuous monitoring of machine identities helps organizations secure their digital ecosystems. By treating all identities—human and non-human—as part of an ongoing governance process, businesses can reduce risks associated with service account sprawl and API-based attacks.

Organizations must embrace a culture of continuous improvement in IGA to keep pace with emerging threats, regulatory shifts, and technological advancements. Establishing governance committees, conducting regular policy reviews, and investing in employee training ensures that identity governance remains aligned with business priorities. Leveraging AI-driven insights, automation, and real-time analytics enables organizations to adapt quickly to changes and maintain a strong security posture. By treating IGA as an ongoing, dynamic process rather than a static implementation, businesses can build resilient, future-proof identity governance frameworks that support growth, innovation, and security.

Final Thoughts: The Future of Identity Governance

Identity Governance and Administration (IGA) has undergone a significant transformation over the past decade, evolving from a compliance-driven function to a critical pillar of cybersecurity strategy. Organizations worldwide recognize the importance of securing digital identities, managing access rights efficiently, and ensuring regulatory compliance. As technology advances, the future of identity governance will be shaped by automation, artificial intelligence, decentralized identity models, and the continuous adaptation of security frameworks to combat emerging threats.

One of the most influential forces driving the future of IGA is artificial intelligence and machine learning. Traditional identity governance models rely heavily on predefined roles, static access controls, and periodic reviews, which can be inefficient and fail to detect real-time security threats. AI-driven IGA solutions enhance security by continuously monitoring user behavior, detecting anomalies, and making real-time access recommendations. As organizations generate vast amounts of identity-related data, machine learning algorithms will play an increasingly critical role in analyzing access patterns, identifying high-risk activities, and automating access decision-making.

The adoption of Zero Trust principles will further reshape identity governance strategies. Unlike traditional perimeter-based security models, Zero Trust operates on the assumption that no user, device, or application should be implicitly trusted. Every access request must be continuously verified based on contextual risk factors, including device health, user behavior, and geolocation. Future IGA frameworks will integrate with Zero Trust security architectures to enforce dynamic access controls, ensure least privilege access, and apply real-time risk scoring to every authentication attempt.

Another significant trend influencing the future of IGA is the shift toward decentralized identity and self-sovereign identity (SSI). Traditional identity management relies on centralized identity providers, which can create security risks and privacy concerns. Decentralized identity models, powered by blockchain technology, will allow individuals to have greater control over their digital identities, reducing reliance on third-party identity providers. By enabling secure, verifiable, and privacy-preserving authentication mechanisms, decentralized identity solutions will enhance security and empower users to manage their credentials with greater autonomy.

The expansion of cloud computing, remote work, and digital collaboration will continue to challenge identity governance strategies. Organizations are moving away from traditional on-premises systems toward hybrid and multi-cloud environments, where users require seamless access to applications across different platforms. Future IGA solutions will need to provide centralized visibility and policy enforcement across on-premises, cloud, and SaaS environments. Federated identity management, identity orchestration, and cloud-native governance solutions will become essential for organizations seeking to maintain control over distributed identity ecosystems.

Regulatory compliance will remain a driving force in the evolution of IGA. As data protection laws become more stringent, organizations must implement identity governance frameworks that align with global compliance standards such as GDPR, HIPAA, SOX, and emerging industry-specific regulations. Future IGA solutions will incorporate automated compliance reporting, continuous access certifications, and AI-driven audit capabilities to help organizations maintain compliance with minimal manual effort. Compliance automation will reduce the administrative burden on security and governance teams while ensuring that identity-related risks are continuously mitigated.

The role of privileged access management (PAM) will expand within the IGA landscape as organizations recognize the growing risk of privileged account misuse. Privileged users, such as IT administrators and executives, have elevated access rights that make them prime targets for cyberattacks. Future IGA solutions will integrate more closely with PAM to enforce just-in-time (JIT) access, session monitoring, and automated privilege escalation controls. By incorporating intelligent risk assessment mechanisms, organizations can ensure that privileged access is granted only when absolutely necessary and revoked immediately after use.

Behavioral analytics will play a key role in the next generation of identity governance solutions. Rather than relying solely on predefined access policies, behavioral analytics will enable organizations to detect unusual access patterns, prevent insider threats, and mitigate account compromise risks. AI-driven anomaly detection will allow organizations to identify deviations from normal user behavior, flag high-risk activities, and trigger automated responses such as step-up authentication, session termination, or access revocation. This proactive approach to identity governance will significantly reduce the risk of identity-related security incidents.

Another emerging trend in identity governance is the integration of identity threat detection and response (ITDR) solutions. As cybercriminals increasingly target identity-based attack vectors, organizations must enhance their ability to detect and respond to identity-related threats in real time. ITDR solutions will provide continuous identity monitoring, advanced forensic capabilities, and automated incident response mechanisms to mitigate credential theft, privilege abuse, and unauthorized access attempts. By incorporating ITDR into IGA frameworks, organizations will be able to respond to identity threats more effectively while minimizing operational disruptions.

User experience and security will need to be balanced in future IGA implementations. Employees, customers, and third-party partners expect seamless, frictionless access to enterprise applications and services without unnecessary security barriers. Adaptive authentication, self-service identity management, and passwordless authentication will become standard features in modern IGA solutions. Organizations that prioritize usability while maintaining strong security controls will improve user satisfaction, reduce IT support costs, and enhance overall operational efficiency.

The convergence of IGA with emerging technologies such as the Internet of Things (IoT), robotic process automation (RPA), and AI-powered digital assistants will introduce new challenges and opportunities in identity governance. Organizations will need to extend identity governance beyond human users to include machine identities, service accounts, and autonomous systems. Implementing governance frameworks that address machine identity lifecycle management, API security, and automated access controls will be critical for securing the next generation of digital ecosystems.

Future-proofing identity governance will require organizations to embrace continuous improvement, automation, and adaptability. IGA must evolve alongside business transformation initiatives, ensuring that security, compliance, and operational efficiency remain aligned with organizational goals. By investing in advanced identity governance technologies, organizations can strengthen security, reduce administrative overhead, and enhance user experiences without compromising on compliance. The evolution of IGA will be defined by its ability to adapt to emerging risks, integrate with new security paradigms, and enable organizations to securely navigate an increasingly complex digital landscape.

www.ingramcontent.com/pod-product-compliance
Lightning Source LLC
LaVergne TN
LVHW022315060326
832902LV00020B/3487